CAN DO

BUILD THE MINDSET, HABITS, AND DISCIPLINE
TO TRANSFORM YOUR LIFE

DANIEL AUSTIN JARVIS

COPYRIGHT PAGE

DEDICATION

To the men and women of the 823d RED HORSE Squadron — the place where I learned discipline, grit, and the true meaning of "Can Do." Your influence is woven into every chapter of this book.

To my family — your love, support, and belief in me have carried me through every season of my life. I am forever grateful.

To Clara Morrell — thank you for the conversation that changed everything. Your encouragement helped me find my way back when I needed it most.

To Andy Frisella — your creation of 75 Hard and the Live Hard Program reshaped my mindset and reminded me what discipline truly looks like.

To Jeremy Mullins — thank you for giving me that extra

push after Clara got me started. Your guidance helped me keep going when momentum mattered most.

To Dr. Blom and Dr. Sheridan — thank you for listening when no one else would. Your willingness to hear me and act on it changed the course of my life.

To Karen Gregory — thank you for pushing me to take the risk of stepping into leadership. Becoming a manager taught me more about emotional intelligence, growth, and self-awareness than I ever expected. Those lessons shaped the way I lead, think, and show up for others.

To the West Virginia Mountain Trail Runners — thank you for supporting the Kanawha Trace 50K/25K/10K, the Moonlight Madness Night Trail Race, and the Darkness Falls Haunted Trail Race. Your community made those events possible and unforgettable.

And finally, to myself — for refusing to quit, for showing up when it was hard, and for doing the work required to become the man I needed to be. This book was a promise I made to myself, and I'm proud that I kept it.

TABLE OF CONTENTS

INTRODUCTION

ABOUT THE AUTHOR

NOTE TO THE READER

This book isn't meant to be read passively. It's meant to be used.

You'll get the most out of CAN DO if you treat it like a conversation — one that challenges you, pushes you, and reminds you of what you're capable of.

You don't need to be perfect. You don't need to have it all figured out. You just need to show up with honesty and a willingness to try. Take what resonates, apply it in small steps, and let the momentum build.

You're not reading this by accident. You're here because a part of you is ready for more.

I'm proud of you for starting.

Let's get to work.

INTRODUCTION

DESIGNING THE PATH TO THE BEST VERSION OF YOU

I grew up in Lesage, West Virginia, in a single-wide trailer tucked into the quiet country. Life was simple back then — pop and Kool-Aid in the fridge, home-cooked meals on the table, and plenty of processed snacks within reach. What we lacked in resources, we made up for in time spent outside. From the moment I could walk, I was playing baseball, and by age four I was on a team. Most days, you could find me and the neighborhood kids running two-on-two games of baseball, basketball, or football until the sun went down. Movement was just part of who I was.

But life has a way of shifting under your feet. My first job at McDonald's introduced me to unlimited soda and fast food, and without the constant activity of childhood, the weight came quickly. College added beer, late nights, and stress. I was working, studying business management at Marshall University, and partying with my fraternity — a cycle that left little room for health.

I made a decision that changed the entire trajectory of my life: I joined the United States Air Force. My first duty station was Hurlburt Field in Florida, where I served in the 823d RED HORSE Squadron— Heavy Operational Repair Squadron Engineers. My AFSC was 3E2X1, Pavements and Heavy Equipment Operator.

The Air Force is built on three core values: Integrity First, Service Before Self, and Excellence in All We Do. The 823d RED HORSE Squadron added its own motto that shaped me just as deeply: "Can Do, Will Do, Have Done."

That mindset stayed with me long after I hung up the uniform. It became part of how I lead, how I work, and how I grow. It's also one of the inspirations behind the title of this book. Can Do is a blend of the values instilled in me during my time with the 823d and the growth-mindset principles I've learned throughout my life. It represents the belief that no matter where you start, you can build discipline, resilience, and the courage to become the best version of yourself.

In the military, I rediscovered exercise and fell in love with running. But even then, I didn't understand nutrition. I could run for miles, but I couldn't outrun a bad diet. Living in the dorms with unlimited food didn't help. My weight went up and down, and I struggled to stay under my maximum allowable weight. It wasn't until I moved into my first apartment and a friend introduced me to the Zone Perfect Diet that I began paying attention to what I put into my body.

My first real wake-up call came after a temporary duty assignment where I ate every meal out. When I returned to base, my bloodwork showed high cholesterol, and I was sent to a dietitian. I learned just enough to bring my numbers down — but not enough to change my life.

I spent my last three years in the Airborne program at Hurlburt Field, jumping out of airplanes, training five days a week, and constantly fighting to stay within weight standards. While attached to the Airborne RED HORSE unit, I also served as the Personnel Parachute Program Manager, responsible for keeping our members jump-qualified. Over that time, I jumped from 31 airplanes and 3 helicopters.

One jump in February 2004 changed everything. We were conducting a routine training mission into Fryar Drop Zone at Fort Benning. As I descended to about a hundred feet, the wind suddenly picked up and blew my body parallel to the ground. Instead of landing on my feet, I struck the ground head-first, was knocked unconscious, and was dragged several hundred yards before I could release my canopy. A black hat was literally riding my parachute like someone skiing behind a boat, yelling for me to pull the release. By the time I stopped, I was covered in mud and had carved a winding trail across the drop zone.

That incident would eventually lead to one of the biggest turning points of my life — something you'll read about later in this introduction.

When my six years of service ended, I made another life-altering decision: I would become a dietitian. I loved cooking, I loved exercise, and I believed I was eating healthy — even though I still had a lot to learn. Then came the moment that reshaped everything.

Around 2018, I noticed swelling on the back of my head. Doctors told me it was lymphedema. Years passed. In 2022, I completed the 75 Hard program and got into the best shape of my life — but the swelling returned. A chiropractor noticed it. Doctors dismissed it again. By November, I could feel it pulsating.

One day at the YMCA, I asked a doctor I knew to check it. He felt it and said, "Yeah, that's vascular." Another doctor — one who treated aneurysms — examined it right there in the locker room and gave me his office number. That moment saved my life.

An ultrasound led to an angiogram, which led to a coil embolization using twelve platinum coils. My aneurysm was treated in February 2023. But recovery wasn't a straight line. Fear held me back.

Pain at the aneurysm site would stop me in my tracks. I'd

start working out, then quit. Add in osteoarthritis, bone spurs, and a meniscus tear, and the setbacks piled up.

A scan in late 2024 revealed another possible aneurysm — likely an imaging artifact, and in a low-risk location — but the worry stayed with me. It still does. Then came August of 2025.

I was talking with my favorite coworker as we worked through a project together. In that conversation, I opened up about my struggles. What she didn't know was that I had quietly given up. I had gone from being in the best shape of my life to weighing even more than I did before starting 75 Hard back in 2022. I felt defeated. I felt old. I wasn't focusing on what I could do — only on what I couldn't.

And because of that, I wasn't doing anything at all.

She told me about the workout program she was doing — mesocycle, three structured strength-training days each week. She shared her plan, and I followed it exactly. Something about that conversation hit differently. I decided to focus on what I could do. I started with band-assisted pull-ups. I had gone from doing 22 pull-ups to barely 5 or 6, but I showed up anyway. Having someone who cared enough to support me and talk training with me helped shift my mindset from can't do to can do.

Before long, I was doing the workouts back-to-back, adding running and walking, and rebuilding my discipline one day at a time. And the rest of the story is still being written. And then something changed.

Instead of stopping when my head hurt, I kept going. Instead of obsessing over what I couldn't do, I leaned into what I could. That mindset shift became the spark. Everything else followed.

Since then, I've lost over twenty pounds, dropped inches off my waist, rebuilt my strength and confidence — and I can now do 32 pull-ups in a row.

And that brings me to my why. I want to be healthy for my family. I want to be strong for my career. I want to live fully for myself. But more than anything, I want to show people something I learned the hard way.

The best version of yourself isn't out there somewhere — it's already inside you. You just have to decide to bring it out. This book is my story, my lessons, and my proof that you can change your life — no matter where you start, no matter what you've been through, and no matter how many times you've fallen down.

This is the journey to becoming your best self.

This is the journey of Can Do.

THE POWER OF "CAN DO"

WHY I STARTED LEARNING ABOUT THE BRAIN

My interest in the brain didn't come from curiosity. It came from survival.

When I had my aneurysm repaired, everything in my life collided at once. I was in a leadership class called *Leading With Values*, and my boss at the time, Brian, had just introduced me to the idea of the amygdala hijack — that moment when emotion overrides logic and you react before you think. I didn't know it then, but that concept would become the anchor for everything I was about to face.

At the same time, I was devouring every book I could find about how the brain works — the chemicals, the circuits, the patterns. And every single one of them talked about the amygdala. Fear. Survival. Reaction. It felt like the universe was preparing me for something I didn't yet understand.

Then the aneurysm happened.

My body didn't feel like my body. My thoughts didn't feel like my thoughts. Every spike in heart rate felt like danger. Every workout felt like a threat. I was living inside a body I no longer trusted, and the fear was constant. It wasn't just in my head — it was in my chest, my breath, my muscles, my heartbeat.

That's when I started listening to Andrew Huberman. I needed answers. I needed to understand what was happening inside me. When he talked about the anterior midcingulate cortex — the part of the brain that grows when you do hard things — it hit me like a lifeline. It gave me a way to understand the fear I was living with and the work I was doing to overcome it.

Around the same time, I was reading David Goggins. Hearing him talk about suffering and resilience landed differently when my own brain had betrayed me. It wasn't motivation. It was validation — proof that the mind could adapt, even after trauma.

And then came exposure therapy.

I spent countless sessions in my backyard, reliving the same HIIT workout over and over. I had to describe everything — what I saw, what I felt, what I feared, what my body was doing, what my mind was screaming. I had to walk through every second of it until my brain finally learned that I was safe.

It was brutal.

It was exhausting.

It was necessary.

And it changed me.

All of it — the leadership training, the amygdala lessons from Brian, the books, the podcasts, the trauma, the fear, the therapy — it was all happening at the same time. It wasn't a neat sequence. It was a storm I had to navigate with no map.

And here's the part I need you to understand: I didn't go back and study all of this again to write this book. I didn't pull out old notes or reread old chapters. I didn't reference anything. This isn't research. This is my core.

And the analogies you're going to read — the fig and the fig wasp, the bucket with holes, the trail runner and the road runner, Groundhog Day, the bull field, PATCH, CODES — none of them were crafted at a desk. They weren't engineered or polished in a classroom. They came from random brainstorms, voice notes, long drives, and moments when I was trying to connect what I was learning with what I was living. They came from trying to make sense of myself.

This book has been a four-year goal — something I've carried through every season of growth, fear, rebuilding, and clarity. And there hasn't been a better time than now to finally write it. Everything in these pages comes from what stayed with me — the things that changed me, the things that scared me, the things that rebuilt me. The things I couldn't forget even if I tried.

That's why the brain shows up in this book. Not because I'm a neuroscientist. But because understanding my brain helped me survive myself. And if it helped me, maybe it can help you too.

From that point on, every lesson, every metaphor, and every breakthrough became part of the path I was carving forward — and that's where this chapter begins.

I didn't know it at the time, but those early moments of trying to make sense of my life — the fear, the rebuilding, the random ideas that hit me while driving or talking out loud — were the beginning of everything you're about to read. I wasn't trying to write a book. I was trying to understand myself. And the only way I knew how was to take the things I was learning, the things I was feeling, and the things I was living, and connect them in ways that made sense to me.

IDENTITY OVER WILLPOWER

Why Discipline Fails When Identity Doesn't Match the Goal

Your identity is always evolving. Every experience, challenge, success, and setback shapes who you are and who you're becoming. The person you are today may not be the person you are tomorrow. That's why one of the most important questions you can ask is: **Who am I becoming?** And just as important: **What am I willing to do to become the best version of myself?**

Discipline alone won't carry you forever. Motivation sparks discipline, and discipline gets you moving — but both fade as life shifts. New circumstances show up. New challenges appear. And when life throws something unexpected at you, your response determines everything. Do you give up on your worst day, or do you keep going?

When my brain aneurysm was discovered, my identity was built on discipline, fortitude, and resilience. I was deep into the Live Hard program, and the habits I built throughout 2022 became the foundation that carried me through the fear of not knowing whether I'd even be here tomorrow. My identity at that time was simple: work hard, train hard, read daily, complete every task, and never quit. That mindset — the identity of doing hard things — is what helped me survive mentally.

But after the aneurysm was repaired, everything shifted. One doctor told me I was fine to work out. Another told me to take it easy. Out of fear, I chose caution. Slowly, the identity I had built through 75 Hard slipped away. My goal of being fit and healthy no longer matched the mindset shaped by the fear of dying during exercise.

For the first few months after surgery, I was afraid to even lay my head on a pillow, worried the platinum coils might shift. Fear ruled me. It dictated my choices. It shaped my identity. Through counseling and exposure therapy, I learned to step in and out of that fear. Some days, it still shows up — especially when I feel pain in the back of my head. I still get checked out for reassurance. That experience changed me forever. But I refuse to let fear define me.

I know who I am. I know who I want to become. And I know what it takes to get there. My identity now aligns with the actions required to be the best version of myself. When identity and action match, willpower becomes almost irrelevant — because you're no longer forcing yourself to change. You're simply acting in alignment with who you truly are.

When you want to become something different than you are today — a runner, a reader, a swimmer, a weightlifter, a cook, a nurse, a dietitian, a scientist, a motivational speaker, a writer — you have to start by thinking like the person you want to become. **Identity comes first. Action follows.**

You won't become a writer overnight. You won't become a swimmer after one lesson. But the moment you take that first step, you ignite the spark that moves you toward that identity. If your goal is to be healthier, fitter, smarter, or more disciplined, then study what those identities require. Build a plan. Take action. And keep showing up.

Before long, you'll realize you're already becoming the best version of yourself — not because of willpower, but because your actions match the identity you've chosen.

Michael Jordan didn't wake up one morning as the greatest basketball player of all time. He became that through years of relentless action. Thomas Edison didn't invent the light bulb on his first attempt. He failed repeatedly, refined his approach, and kept going. He became an inventor because he did what inventors do: create, fail, recreate, and persist until the goal is achieved.

Whatever identity you seek, the path is the same:

Choose the identity.

Take the actions that identity requires.

Repeat them until they become who you are.

That's how transformation happens.

How to Shift From "Trying" to Becoming

Think about all the times you've tried something new. How often did you enjoy it the first time? And when you didn't enjoy it, did you go back and try again? Or did you walk away because it felt hard, uncomfortable, or because you didn't meet your expectations right out of the gate?

When you're building a new identity, you create a list of actions that identity requires. But the moment you stop taking those actions — for any reason — you stop moving toward that identity. "Trying" becomes quitting.

If you want to become, you can't stop at trying. You keep showing up. You keep taking action, even when you're not good at it yet. Everyone starts as an apprentice before they ever become a craftsman or an expert.

Every time you do something difficult — especially when you don't feel like doing it — you strengthen a part of the brain called the anterior mid-cingulate cortex, the region responsible for grit, persistence, and doing hard things. If you truly want to become the best version of yourself, you must take action even on the days you don't want to. That is discipline. And discipline is the bridge between trying and becoming.

Eventually, trying turns into doing. And the more you do it, the easier it becomes. Not only are you strengthening the anterior mid-cingulate cortex, you're also forging new neural pathways through neuroplasticity and adding myelin to your neurons — making those pathways faster, stronger, and more automatic.

Your body responds too. Every time you take action, you trigger chemical messengers like dopamine, oxytocin, epinephrine, and serotonin. Each plays a role in motivation, connection, energy, and well-being. When you understand what stimulates these chemicals, you can use them to support your growth and build a powerful internal toolbelt.

Becoming isn't about perfection. It's about repetition. It's about identity. It's about choosing the new path again and again until it becomes who you are.

When you want to build muscle, you go to the gym. You lift weights. Then you come back the next day and lift again. And again. If you want to get good at lifting weights, you don't just show up — you study the craft. You read books on strength training. You might hire a personal trainer. You might take a class or watch instructional videos.

These are the action steps that move you from trying to be a weightlifter to becoming one. Most weightlifters share a common goal: building muscle — and building it evenly. To do that, you have to master different exercises, choose the right weights, and understand how to balance training with rest, sleep, and nutrition. It's a full process. It's a mindset. And it takes time.

Patience becomes part of the journey. Consistent action,

repeated over weeks and months, is what produces results. They won't show up overnight. In the beginning, you'll feel the frustration of waiting for progress that hasn't revealed itself yet. That's normal.

The key is not giving up. Keep showing up. Keep taking the steps. Keep choosing the identity of a weightlifter — even before you feel like one. Over time, the results will come, and you'll realize you didn't just build muscle. You built the identity that made it possible.

The Science of Identity-Based Habits

Identity-based habits are built by looking at your current behaviors and letting them shape the identity you want to grow into. As we talked about earlier, if you want to become a runner, you must take the actions a runner takes.

What does a runner do? They run. And if you've never run before, you start slow. You build strength in your legs, core, lungs, and arms. You choose the right shoes for your feet, the right clothes for the weather, and a safe path to run on. Then you run again. And again. And again. Over time, the repetition forms the identity. Eventually, you don't just run — **you are a runner.**

It also helps to call yourself one. When someone asks what you enjoy doing, say, "I'm a runner," not "I like to run." One is an activity. The other is an identity. And identity is what sticks.

No matter what identity you're trying to build, the most

powerful thing you can do is refer to yourself as the person you want to become. Your words reinforce your actions, and your actions reinforce your identity. That's how transformation takes root.

When people think of runners, they often picture Usain Bolt — the fastest human on the planet. Others imagine marathoners, ultra-runners, or athletes who glide through 5Ks without breaking a sweat. But runners come in every shape, size, age, and ability. Being a runner doesn't mean you have to sprint like Bolt or log daily marathons like Dean Karnazes. You don't even have to be good at running to call yourself a runner.

When I think of runners, I don't just think of the elites. I think of myself. I think of Robert Smith, Dan Green, and Bob Luther — incredible runners in our community who show up with heart, consistency, and grit. Dan Green even became a professional runner, and all three of them inspire others simply by doing the work day after day. They remind me that running isn't defined by speed or distance. It's defined by commitment, by showing up, and by the willingness to keep moving forward.

These are the runners who prove that identity is built through action — one step, one mile, one choice at a time. You simply have to take the actions runners take. You lace up your shoes. You step outside. You run — at your pace, at your level, with your effort. And you keep doing it. Over time, those actions shape your identity. You begin to think like a runner, act like a runner, and carry the mindset of someone who doesn't quit.

That's the essence of identity-based change: **you become the person you repeatedly choose to be.**

3

DISCIPLINE IS A SKILL

The idea of "naturally disciplined people" is a myth. No one is born with discipline, and it doesn't suddenly appear one day. Discipline is a skill — a way of living — that is built through repeated action over time. It begins early in life, long before we're aware of it. We learn discipline by watching, listening, touching, and mimicking the people around us. This is where mirror neurons come into play. We subconsciously copy the behaviors of our family and culture — how they eat, how they move, how they respond to stress — and those patterns become the earliest versions of our habits.

The more we repeat a behavior, the easier it becomes to repeat again. Each repetition adds another layer of myelin to the neurons involved, strengthening that pathway through neuroplasticity. Some of the earliest examples of discipline are learning to crawl, walk, and talk. None of those skills came naturally. They were built through repetition — through trying, failing, and trying again until the action became second nature. Through this process, the brain forms new pathways, and those pathways become the foundation for future habits.

Discipline is deeply connected to our neurons and the chemicals they release. These chemicals reinforce behaviors by creating feelings that reward us and increase our chances of survival. In many ways, discipline is rooted in our survival instincts. It's the brain's way of saying, "This matters. Do it again." That's why elite performers like Tom Brady and Stephen Curry didn't become great by accident. Brady's TB12 method involves training four to five times a week, and Curry takes roughly 500 shots a day. Their excellence was built through years of disciplined repetition, not natural talent alone.

Repetition builds discipline, but repetition by itself isn't enough. When progress is slow and the reward isn't obvious, something else has to keep you moving. That "something" is the reward system you build for yourself — the benefits you choose to value. The reward might be physical, emotional, or deeply internal, but whatever it is, it has to matter to you. It also has to be flexible. Discipline collapses when the reward is rigid and thrives when the incentive can shift and adapt as you grow. Sometimes the reward is progress. Sometimes it's pride. Sometimes it's simply knowing you didn't quit today.

Understanding what motivates you — and allowing that motivation to evolve — is what keeps you aligned with the identity you're trying to build.

This is how champions stay consistent. This is how discipline becomes a lifestyle. Every time you do something difficult, especially when you don't feel like doing it, you strengthen the anterior midcingulate cortex — the part of the brain responsible for grit, persistence, and doing hard things. That's why the first step in building discipline is often just going through the motions. You don't wait for motivation. You act, and the brain adapts.

A simple example is drinking more water. Start by asking yourself how much water you currently drink and how much you want to drink each day. Then make it easy: fill a container with your daily goal and keep it visible. If you can see the water, you're more likely to drink it. Do this every day, and over time it becomes automatic. The timeline varies for everyone, but the key is consistency — showing up every day with discipline. Visualization can help too. Imagine yourself filling the bottle, drinking from it, watching the level drop, and finishing it completely. The more you visualize the action, the more likely you are to follow through. When something stays active in your mind, action eventually follows.

I used visualization heavily when training for the Kanawha Trace 50K. I wrote out the entire course in sections and read through it every day, imagining myself running each part of the trail. I wrote down strength training goals and pictured myself lifting weights, doing squats, deadlifts, and bench presses. I imagined my waist shrinking, my muscles tightening, and my body getting leaner. I saw the results long before they appeared. Visualization primes your brain, repetition strengthens your pathways, and action transforms your identity. Change happens one thought, one repetition, and one choice at a time.

Micro-discipline plays a huge role in this process. We often get so focused on the end result that we quit when progress doesn't show up fast enough. Breaking big goals into smaller, manageable pieces helps you stay in the game. If your goal is to lose 40 pounds, it's easy to fixate on that final number and hope it happens quickly. But when the scale doesn't move as fast as you want, frustration sets in — and that's when most people quit. Small wins keep you moving. Pay attention to how your clothes fit. Measure your waist, arms, and hips. Notice improvements in energy, sleep, strength, or mood. It may have taken months or years to gain the weight, so losing it will take time too. Celebrating small wins keeps you engaged long enough to reach the bigger goal.

Small wins build momentum. Momentum builds consistency. Consistency creates results. And that's how you stay in the game long enough to reach the finish line.

4

THE ART OF SHOWING UP

Why Consistency Beats Intensity

When you start something new — strength training, running, swimming, reading, volunteering — the most important part is simply showing up. Showing up every day outlasts any single hard workout, any fast run, or any marathon reading session. Anyone can show up once and crush a workout, run their fastest mile, or read until they fall asleep. But the real question is whether you can show up on the days when you can't run fast, when the workout feels heavy, or when you only have the energy to read a few pages. If you choose to show up, you've already done something. And doing something day after day is what creates results over time. When you don't show up, you gain nothing. You don't have to be at your best to become your best. You don't have to outperform your best day every day. The people who show up consistently — even at 50% — will always outperform the person who goes all-out once or twice a year and disappears the rest of the time.

Fat loss is a perfect example. It takes 3,500 kilocalories to burn one pound of fat. You're not going to burn 3,500 calories in a single day unless you're running an ultramarathon — and even then, you're eating along the way just to keep moving. But burning just 100–200 calories a day adds up. Over time, those small daily efforts compound. One hundred calories burned each day becomes 36,500 calories in a year. Divide that by 3,500, and you get 10.43 pounds of fat lost. That's the power of showing up. You might not notice losing 0.86 pounds a month. It's subtle. But if you take progress photos every few weeks, you'll see the difference — assuming you're not eating back the calories you burn. Small, consistent actions create big results over time.

The same principle applies to reading. If you read just five pages a day for an entire year, that's 1,825 pages. A typical self-help book is 150–170 pages. A full-length nonfiction book is 220–250 pages. A research-heavy nonfiction book is 300 pages or more. With five pages a day, you could finish ten to twelve self-help books, seven to eight full-length nonfiction books, or six research-heavy books. All from five pages a day. And if you read ten pages a day? Or fifteen? The number of books you could finish — and the amount of knowledge you could absorb — becomes incredible. And it all starts with showing up for a few minutes each day.

This principle applies everywhere: burning 100–200 calories a day, walking a mile, doing a short workout, practicing a skill for ten minutes. Small, consistent actions compound over time. Five pages a day doesn't feel like much — until you look back and realize how far it carried you. Showing up is the secret. Showing up is the advantage. Showing up is the transformation.

The Sponge Analogy: Why Showing Up Works

Whenever you're working with someone — a patient, a coworker, a friend, or even yourself — remember the sponge. We all absorb information differently. Some people have a big sponge. Some have a small one. Some soak things up quickly. Others need time to wring things out before they can take in more. And here's the key: people learn better when they have choices.

Think about kids in a grocery store. The moment they walk in, they're excited because they know they might get to choose something. That choice is the trigger. It creates motivation. Adults aren't any different. When we choose what we want to learn or work on, we get excited about it. But even with excitement, a sponge can only hold so much. If you try to clean up four messes at once with one sponge, you're going to make a bigger mess. But if you clean one spill at a time — soak it up, wring it out, go back again — eventually the whole counter is clean.

Learning works the same way. Habits work the same way. Growth works the same way. Sometimes you have to talk to a patient two or three times about phosphorus before it sticks. Not because they're not trying — but because their sponge is full. They need time to wring it out. And the same is true for you. Don't try to fix everything at once. Pick one mess. One habit. One change. Soak it up. Wring it out. Repeat. That's how real growth happens — and that's why showing up matters more than intensity.

Groundhog Day and the Power of Repetition

One of my favorite movies of all time is *Groundhog Day* — a story about a man who starts out bitter, sarcastic, lonely, and stuck in a cycle of complacency. He wasn't always that way, but life wore him down. What makes this movie powerful is that it becomes a story of personal growth, transformation, and identity. It captures everything it means to become the best version of yourself.

Phil Connors, a Pittsburgh TV weatherman, finds himself reliving the same day — February 2nd — over and over again. Some estimates suggest he may have repeated that day for 10 to 30 years based on the skills he mastered by the end. Think about that: years of repetition, years of practice, years of refining himself one small action at a time. As Phil begins to embrace the situation instead of fighting it, he transforms. He stops wasting the day and starts using it. He learns new skills. He helps people. He becomes kinder, more patient, more intentional. He becomes someone worth becoming.

And here's the truth: we all have our own version of *Groundhog Day*. We wake up with the same 24 hours. We face the same routines. We encounter the same opportunities to grow — or the same temptations to procrastinate. We won't suddenly wake up with new abilities like Phil appears to on that final day, but we can start small. We can download an app and practice singing. We can buy a guitar and take lessons. We can show up at the gym and lift weights until one day we realize we've become a weightlifter. All it takes is choosing to live each day with intention — putting your best foot forward and stopping procrastination before it stops you.

Be like Phil. Take the opportunity to grow. Become the best version of yourself. Learn something new. Try something uncomfortable. Take a chance on love. Take a chance on yourself. And hopefully, it won't take you as long as it took Phil to get things right. But even if it does, persistence and resilience will carry you farther than intensity ever will. Showing up — day after day — is what transforms you. That's how you break the cycle. That's how you build identity. That's how you become who you were meant to be.

5

REMOVING FRICTION

How Your Environment Shapes Your Behavior

Your environment shapes your behavior more than you realize. Imagine starting in the perfect environment: you have time, support, resources, good health, and a clear path forward. In that situation, success feels almost inevitable. But most people don't start there. Some have time but no support. Some have support but no time. Some have both, but lack the resources to buy the foods or tools they need. Some have everything — except their health has slipped so far that starting feels overwhelming. Environment matters. It can lift you up or weigh you down. But recognizing your environment is the first step to working with it instead of against it. Even if your starting point isn't perfect, you can still build momentum. You can still create change. You can still become the healthiest, strongest version of yourself — no matter where you begin.

When You Have No Support

Sometimes the hardest part of starting a new journey is realizing you don't have the support you hoped for. When that happens, the first step is vulnerability. Let the people in your life know how you feel. Tell them — calmly and without confrontation — that their support matters to you and that you'd like them on your side. Often, people don't realize the impact their silence or indifference has until you share it.

But what if you've tried that and nothing changes? Then you move forward anyway. You acknowledge the lack of support, set it aside, and take action for yourself. That might mean waking up early to get your workout in before anyone else is awake. It might mean preparing your own meals even if no one else is eating the way you are. As long as your why is strong and rooted in something meaningful, you can keep going without applause.

And here's the beautiful part: support often shows up later. People notice consistency. They notice effort. They notice when you keep showing up, even without encouragement. Over time, the same people who didn't support you at first may start to admire your discipline — and some may even join you. Be the example others aspire to. Lead by action, not permission. When you do that, you haven't just gained support — you've earned it.

When You Think You Have No Time

When you feel like you have no time, the first question to ask is: *Is that really true?* Often, the problem isn't a lack of time — it's a lack of clarity about how your time is being used. Start by creating a visual map of your day. Lay out everything you do from the moment you wake up to the moment you go to bed. Then highlight the activities that genuinely add value to your life — the things that support your goals, your health, your relationships, and your purpose.

Next, take an honest look at the time wasters: scrolling social media, watching TV without really watching, sleeping more than your body needs, drifting through the day without intention. The key is to build a process that supports the life you want. Keep the activities that add value, and reduce — or eliminate — the ones that don't. Reclaim that time and give it back to yourself, your goals, and your why.

You don't need more hours in the day. You need to redirect the hours you already have. When you do that, you'll discover you have far more time than you realized — and you can finally use it to build the life you're working toward.

When You Don't Have the Resources

If you feel like you can't afford healthy food, the first step is to take an honest look at your budget. You might discover you're paying for multiple streaming services you barely use. Maybe you're buying the most expensive version of products when a more affordable option works just as well. Maybe you're not choosing produce that's in season, which is almost always cheaper.

And sometimes, if we're being honest, "eating healthy is too expensive" becomes an easy excuse. A bag of apples costs around five dollars and can last a single person more than a week. A bag of nacho chips costs the same — sometimes more — and can disappear in minutes. Eating healthy doesn't mean buying specialty items or trendy foods. It means choosing whole foods, buying produce in season, and eating appropriate portions. You'd be surprised how little you actually need to meet your nutritional needs.

If you've trimmed your budget, made smart choices, and still struggle to afford food, that's not a failure — that's food insecurity. And there are resources available. Local churches, food banks, and community organizations can help. Websites like Aunt Bertha can connect you with programs designed to make sure you have access to healthy food and a stable foundation.

When You're Not in Good Health

If you're not in the best health before beginning your transformation, the first step is to make sure you're safe. Talk with your doctor and confirm that the changes you want to make are appropriate for your current condition. From there, ask for referrals to professionals who can guide you: a Registered Dietitian to help you navigate nutrition, a personal trainer to design safe workouts, or a physical therapist if you have injuries or limitations that need special attention.

The goal is to cover your bases and gather the best advice you can. When you understand your body, your limitations, and your needs, you can start your journey with confidence — and focus on what you *can* do. Every step forward counts. Starting safely sets you up for long-term success.

Eliminating Triggers That Lead to Bad Habits

We all have triggers — cues we've reinforced over the years through repetition and deeply myelinated neural pathways. These triggers are strong, automatic, and often hard to break away from. That's why the simplest and most effective strategy is to keep them out of sight and out of mind. If certain foods tempt you, don't bring them into the house. If you mindlessly eat in front of the TV, don't eat during that activity. If gaming leads to snacking, limit the time or change the environment.

Some triggers are emotional: a certain day, a certain smell, or a certain routine that sparks cravings for ice cream, pizza, fried chicken, candy, soda — or in your case, Sour Patch Kids at the movies with popcorn and a Coke Zero. Sometimes just thinking about the movie theater flips that switch.

The key is identifying your triggers and creating a plan to avoid or interrupt them. If you do buy something unhealthy, put it in the highest cabinet or the hardest-to-reach spot. But hiding the trigger is only part of the solution. The real transformation happens when you replace the bad habit with a good one. When a trigger fires, use it as a cue to practice a positive behavior. Each time you choose the new habit, you're carving a fresh neural pathway. Repeat it enough, and you begin to myelinate that new pathway until it becomes the dominant one.

The old habits never fully disappear — they lie dormant, waiting for the right moment to resurface. Your job is to keep strengthening the new pathways so the old ones stay quiet. Consistency rewires the brain. Repetition builds identity. Eliminating triggers gives you the space to become who you're trying to be.

Designing Your Surroundings for Success

Designing your surroundings for success can take many forms. For some, it means signing up for a gym and committing to showing up. For others, it might be buying a few pieces of exercise equipment and setting up a small workout space in the garage. Maybe it's stepping out your front door for a run around the neighborhood, or even choosing to live closer to a park with running trails. Your environment can be shaped in countless ways — but it always starts with intention.

And designing your surroundings isn't just about physical objects. It's also about the people you choose to spend your time with. If your closest friends spend their evenings watching TV, drinking soda, eating pizza and candy, and dismissing healthy habits as "crazy," you're not setting yourself up for success. You can still spend time with them, but be the example. Bring healthier snacks. Suggest a walk. Show them what's possible. Let your actions speak for what you value.

But when you're serious about becoming better, seek out people who are already doing the things you want to do. Surround yourself with runners, lifters, readers, creators — people who live the lifestyle you're trying to build. The more you do the same actions they do, the more you grow. Eventually, you may even surpass the people you once looked up to, and you'll find yourself seeking a new circle that challenges you again.

Growth introduces you to people at every stage of their own journey. Learn from them. Support them. Improve together. Then find the next person who pushes you to rise even higher. Design your surroundings with purpose, and your surroundings will shape you into the person you're becoming.

6

UNDERSTANDING YOUR HABIT LOOPS

The Cue → Routine → Reward Cycle

Every habit you have — good or bad — follows the same pattern: **cue → routine → reward.** To change a habit, you first have to understand this loop. Start by listing the habits you want to change, then break each one down into the cue (the trigger), the routine (the action), and the reward (the feeling or chemical release that reinforces it). Once you understand the loop, you can begin to rewrite it.

The Cue

A cue is anything that triggers a behavior. It can be something you see, hear, smell, touch, or taste. Cues can also be emotional — boredom, stress, excitement, loneliness — anything that pushes you toward a familiar routine. Imagine driving down the road and catching the aroma of your favorite restaurant drifting through the window. That smell is the cue. The routine is pulling in and ordering food. The reward is the taste — and the chemical release that comes with it. Oxytocin, often called the "love chemical," is tied to bonding, comfort, and emotional connection. That's part of why eating at your favorite restaurant feels so good — it's not just the food, it's the emotional reward. It's also why dinner dates are so common: good food paired with good company amplifies the feeling of connection.

Roller coasters follow the same pattern. The cue is the sight of the ride, the routine is getting on, and the reward is the surge of epinephrine — adrenaline — that creates the thrill people chase. Music works the same way. When you hear your favorite song, dopamine is released. Dopamine is tied to anticipation and reward, the "I want more of that" chemical. The more you listen, the more your brain associates that song with pleasure, and the more you seek it out.

Social connection has its own loop as well. Think about a close friend you haven't seen in a while. When you find out they're coming to town, you feel excitement, warmth, and anticipation — all tied to serotonin, the chemical associated with well-being and happiness. These loops are everywhere, and once you see them, you can't unsee them.

Why This Matters for Breaking Bad Habits

Once you understand the cue → routine → reward loop, you can start to interrupt it. When you recognize the cue for a habit you want to break, you can immediately redirect yourself into a positive behavior instead. This is how neuroplasticity works: every time you choose a new routine, you begin forming a new neural pathway. Repeat it enough, and you strengthen that pathway through myelination. Eventually, the new habit becomes the automatic one. You're not fighting the cue — you're rewiring the routine. That's how you take control of your habits, your behaviors, and ultimately, your identity.

Why Bad Habits Feel Automatic

Bad habits feel automatic because, at a neurological level, they are. Over years — sometimes decades — you've built strong neural pathways around those behaviors. Each repetition adds more myelin to the neurons involved, making the pathway faster, smoother, and easier for your brain to choose. The more you perform a habit, the more automatic it becomes. And sometimes you know you're engaging in a bad habit... and you do it anyway. That's not weakness — that's wiring.

Identifying Your Personal Triggers

I lived this firsthand. During the period when my doctor restricted me from working out, I slipped into the mindset of "you only live once." I chased every food I had been avoiding. The moment I tasted that first Sour Patch Kid, the floodgates opened. Ice cream, French fries, pizza — all the foods I used to love but knew weren't serving me — came rushing back into my routine.

Looking back, I understand exactly why it happened. I was getting a double hit of brain chemistry: oxytocin, which gave me comfort and emotional warmth, and epinephrine, the thrill of doing something I "shouldn't." That combination created a powerful emotional cocktail. And like any strong habit loop, it pulled me in deeper until I had gained over twenty pounds and hit one of the lowest points in my journey.

But that low point became a turning point. Around that time, I found myself having conversation after conversation with my friend and coworker, Clara. I kept telling her how out of shape I felt, how old I felt, how far I'd drifted from the person I wanted to be. She listened — really listened — and then gave me exactly what I needed: honesty, encouragement, and support. She told me to just start doing something again. Anything. Lift a little. Move a little. Begin where I was, not where I used to be. Then she shared her workout routine with me — Meso-cycle 1, 2, and 3 — and that structure gave me a place to start.

Once I began moving again, I started paying attention to my triggers — the cues that had been pulling me back into old habits. Instead of letting them control me, I replaced them with healthier versions. Instead of ordering pizza, I made a small high-fiber tortilla with a little sauce and cheese. It still gave me that familiar oxytocin comfort, and I even felt a spark of epinephrine — the thrill of finding a better way. That tiny shift became a new routine, and that new routine started forming a new pathway.

Sometimes the people who help you the most have no idea how big of an impact they've made. Clara was that person for me. She didn't just give me a workout plan — she gave me belief, direction, and the push I desperately needed. I'm forever grateful to her for helping me find my way back.

That's how new habits begin: by identifying the cue and rewriting the routine. And the more you repeat that new routine, the stronger and more automatic it becomes — until one day, the healthy choice is the one your brain reaches for without hesitation.

7

MANAGING THE WITHDRAWAL LOOP

H ow to Build a Replacement Routine That Doesn't Shock the Brain

When you decide to quit a bad habit, the instinct is often to eliminate it completely — to stop doing it altogether and hope the behavior simply disappears. But quitting cold turkey rarely works because your brain isn't just losing a habit; it's losing the chemical rewards that habit used to provide. When someone suddenly stops drinking soda, eating fast food, smoking, scrolling social media — anything that once brought comfort or stimulation — the brain reacts. Internal cues fire. Cravings intensify. And the withdrawal loop kicks in. To understand why this happens, you have to understand the chemistry behind your habits.

The CODES Chemistry Behind Every Habit

Your brain releases a cluster of chemicals every time you

perform a familiar behavior. I call this cluster **CODES**, because each letter represents a chemical tied to the habit loop:

Cortisol — the stress chemical

Oxytocin — the comfort and bonding chemical

Dopamine — the anticipation and reward chemical

Epinephrine — the thrill chemical

Serotonin — the well-being and stability chemical

These chemicals are the reason habits feel good, familiar, comforting, exciting, or stabilizing. And when you quit cold turkey, your brain suddenly loses access to all of them at once.

Why Cold Turkey Fails

Imagine being prescribed all five of these chemicals every day — then having them taken away overnight. You'd feel irritable, restless, emotional, stressed, and unbalanced. That's exactly what happens when you remove a habit without replacing it. Dopamine drops, so cravings spike because the brain isn't getting its expected reward. Serotonin dips, especially if the habit regulated your mood. Oxytocin disappears, removing comfort and emotional soothing. Epinephrine fades, leaving you bored or restless. Cortisol rises, because your brain just lost a predictable coping mechanism. This chemical storm is why people relapse. It's not weakness — it's biology.

The Bucket with Holes

Sometimes the withdrawal loop isn't about discipline or

motivation. Sometimes the real problem is that you're trying to fill a bucket that's full of holes. You pour in effort. You pour in willpower. You pour in new habits, new routines, new goals. And it all leaks out. Not because you're failing — but because your brain is overwhelmed.

When you try to quit multiple habits at once, start multiple new routines, or overhaul your entire life overnight, your dopamine leaks out through every hole. Your "happy chemicals" drain faster than you can refill them. That's why you feel stuck. That's why you feel exhausted. That's why nothing seems to work. Your bucket isn't broken. It's just leaking.

And that's where your trusty Flex Seal comes in — the **P.A.T.C.H. method.**

P.A.T.C.H. — How to Fix a Leaky Bucket

P — Pause and identify the leak.

Your brain can't patch ten leaks at once. Choose the one habit that's draining you the most.

A — Accept the challenge.

Stop avoiding it. Stop pretending it's not a problem. Own the leak so you can fix it.

T — Tackle it one step at a time.

Small steps. Repeatable steps. Steps your brain can actually handle without burning out.

C — Create a plan you can stick to, not a fantasy plan.

A real plan. One that fits your life, your energy, and your season.

H — Hang up the bucket and examine it for holes.

Pause and reflect. Look honestly at your life. Where else are you leaking? Where else are you overwhelmed, overstimulated, or overcommitted? You can't fix what you refuse to look at. Patch the holes, and suddenly everything you pour in starts to count.

What Happens After You Patch the Bucket

Once you've patched the bucket, you stop trying to change everything at once. You stop chasing dopamine through chaos. You start working with your brain instead of against it. And that's where tapering comes in.

Instead of going from three diet sodas a day to zero overnight, you taper:

3 per day

2.5

2

1.5

1

0.5

Zero

Spread this over a few weeks, and your brain adjusts gradually. The sudden crash of dopamine, oxytocin, epinephrine, and serotonin never hits all at once. Cortisol doesn't spike as dramatically. And the withdrawal loop becomes manageable instead of overwhelming.

8

THE PSYCHOLOGY
OF SELF-SABOTAGE

Why We Sabotage Progress Even When We Want Change

I've lost count of how many times I've started over. I've gone from being in great shape to being completely out of shape more times than I can remember. Some of those setbacks had valid reasons behind them. Others were moments where I could have focused on what I *could* do instead of what I couldn't. But the pattern was always the same: I made progress, then I sabotaged it.

One of the earliest examples was in 2005, right after I left the Air Force. I moved back to West Virginia from Florida and planned to start school in the fall to become a dietitian. With the whole summer free, I started running at Ritter Park — 2.5 miles out, 2.5 miles back. I felt strong and proud of myself. And then I'd go home and eat an entire pizza. I was building a good habit and destroying it in the same breath. Looking back now, I could have had one slice and stopped, but at the time I didn't understand the emotional patterns driving my choices.

As the months went on, I kept running and slowly started eating healthier. But once school started, everything changed. I stopped exercising, started gaining weight, and fell into a routine of going to class, eating, studying, and sleeping. During my dietetic internship, I worked weekends at Cabell Huntington Hospital and interned during the week. There was no time for anything else. My health took a back seat.

After graduation, I made it my mission to get back in shape. I moved next door to the YMCA, walked over every day, and ran from my apartment to Ritter Park. I got lean, strong, and eventually started running marathons. For several years, I was in the best shape of my life. Then life shifted again. I got married, became a race director for four different races, and suddenly my running stopped. I poured everything into work, marriage, new babies, and the races. I neglected myself completely. And once again, I sabotaged my progress.

Eventually, something clicked. I realized I needed to take care of myself first so I could take care of everyone else better. I got back on track and was doing great — until travel cheer and then travel volleyball took over. My routine fell apart, and the weight came back. In 2022, I completed 75 Hard and the entire Live Hard program. I ended the year feeling unstoppable — until I was diagnosed with an unruptured brain aneurysm. It was repaired in 2023, but the fear of working out again held me back. I sabotaged all the progress I had fought so hard for.

And then came the moment that changed everything again: a simple conversation with Clara. Something in that conversation flipped a switch. I stopped letting fear and excuses run the show, and I got back to work.

Why We Sabotage Ourselves Even When We Want Change

People assume self-sabotage happens because we're lazy or unmotivated, but that's not the real reason. The truth is much more uncomfortable: we're afraid of what it will take to maintain the better version of ourselves. Improvement feels exciting at first. You get momentum, you feel proud, you start to see progress. But then a deeper fear creeps in — the fear that if you keep going, you'll have to keep going. You'll have to live at that higher standard every day. You'll have to keep showing up, keep doing the work, keep proving it to yourself.

Most people have a natural resistance to anything that requires extra effort. Not because they don't want to grow, but because growth demands consistency. And consistency demands identity. When you become better, you raise your own expectations. You can't hide behind the old version of yourself anymore. You can't say, "I'm just not that person." You *are* that person now — and that responsibility scares people. So they pull back. They slip. They sabotage. Not because they don't want the goal, but because they're afraid of the responsibility that comes with achieving it.

It takes a powerful why — a deeply personal reason — to push through that resistance and keep doing the extra work required to stay better.

Emotional Patterns That Keep People Stuck

Self-sabotage isn't random. It follows predictable emotional patterns rooted in the amygdala — the part of the brain wired for fear, comfort, and survival. When the amygdala takes over, you get stuck in an "amygdala hijack," reacting emotionally instead of acting intentionally.

The Opossum, the Fox, and the Raccoon

When we get hit with something stressful or unexpected, we don't always respond like the best version of ourselves. Sometimes we respond like animals in the wild — instinctively, reactively, and without thinking. And depending on the situation, we can slip into one of three modes.

Sometimes we play dead like an opossum. When a situation feels overwhelming or uncomfortable, we shut down. We freeze. We go quiet. We pretend we don't exist. It's not weakness — it's biology. It's our brain buying time so we don't make things worse. And honestly, starting with the opossum response is usually the smartest move. It gives you a moment to pause, breathe, and let the amygdala settle so you can think clearly.

If you don't pause, things can get messy — like a raccoon.

The raccoon reacts fast, loud, and chaotic. That's what happens when the amygdala hijack takes over. You jump into the situation without thinking. You claw at the problem. You make noise. You make a mess. And afterward, you're left cleaning up the emotional trash you scattered everywhere.

But when you pause first, you get to choose the fox. The fox is strategic. The fox is intentional. The fox moves with purpose, not panic. When you start with the opossum — the pause — you give yourself the chance to shift into the fox — the plan. So don't let the amygdala hijack turn you into the raccoon. Start like the opossum. Then move like the fox. And if you're not sure what to do next... ask the fox what he would say. Because the fox always answers with strategy, not emotion.

Four Patterns That Trigger the Opossum Response

Assumptions That Limit Identity

People make quiet assumptions about themselves that become invisible walls: *I'm not good enough. I'm not a runner. I'm too big to exercise. I'm too old to start. People will laugh at me.* These assumptions feel like facts, but they're just fears dressed up as truth.

Self-Criticizing Thoughts

Negative self-talk is one of the strongest forms of sabotage: *You're too slow. You can't lift weights. You're not smart enough to finish your degree. You don't have time to work out.* The irony is that most people do have time — they just don't believe they're worth the effort.

The Victim Mindset

This pattern turns every obstacle into a reason to quit: *Every time I want to run, it rains. Something always gets in the way. I just can't catch a break.* The victim mindset removes responsibility — but it also removes power.

Returning to Comfort

When discomfort shows up — physical, emotional, or mental — people retreat to what feels familiar: the couch, the TV, the snacks, the routine that keeps them stuck. Comfort becomes the reward, even when it leads to frustration or stagnation.

These patterns don't mean someone is weak. They mean their brain is doing what it's wired to do: avoid discomfort, avoid risk, avoid change. But once you understand these patterns, you can interrupt them — and that's where transformation begins.

Strategies to Break the Cycle

Every emotional pattern — assumptions, self-criticism, victimhood, comfort-seeking — can be interrupted. And it all begins with one simple action: pause. Reflect. Let your prefrontal cortex step in. When you pause, you interrupt the amygdala hijack. You stop reacting and start reasoning.

Challenge your assumptions. Ask: *Is this actually true? Does this thought make sense? Is this reality, or fear talking?* Most assumptions collapse under the weight of honesty.

Redirect self-criticism. Shift from "I can't" to "What can

I do right now?" Self-criticism freezes you. Self-support moves you forward.

Stop playing the victim — advocate for yourself. If it rains, run in the rain. If something gets in the way, find a workaround. If life pushes back, push back harder.

Question your comfort. Ask: *Is this the version of myself I want to see in the mirror every day?* Comfort isn't the enemy — but comfort as a default becomes a trap.

Self-sabotage isn't a character flaw — it's a pattern. And patterns can be changed. The moment you choose awareness over autopilot, you break the cycle. And once you break it even once, you prove to yourself that you're capable of becoming someone new.

9

HOVER — THE SPACE BETWEEN INTENTION AND ACTION

HOVER — The Space Between Intention and Action

Hover is the space between who we are and who we could be. It's the invisible gap between the active phase of our goals and the pre-contemplation stage where nothing has begun. Hover is stagnation — standing at the edge of a cliff with a hang glider strapped to your back, knowing you could soar, but never taking the step forward. It's latent potential, the action that never happened, the version of you that never emerged. When we hover, we shut down our aspirations. We hold ourselves back for reasons that feel valid in the moment but ultimately keep us from becoming who we were meant to be.

To break out of hover, we need three things: a clear **why**, a defined **how**, and a committed **when.** Your why gives you direction. Your how gives you structure. Your when puts you into motion. Without all three, you stay hovering.

H — Holding Yourself Back

The first letter in HOVER stands for Holding Yourself Back — and holding yourself back almost always shows up as excuses. Whenever you hear yourself say the word "but...," pay attention. "But" is the gateway to the excuse that follows. "I want to get in shape, but I'm too busy." "I want to start that project, but I don't know where to begin." "I want to change, but I'm not ready." The moment you say "but," you've already decided to stay where you are.

Breaking out of the H phase begins with awareness. Write down every excuse you make. Catch yourself when you say "but." Replace "but" with silence and let that silence become reflection. Crush the excuse before it becomes a belief, and replace it with a proactive, encouraging statement. Holding back is nothing more than a list of reasons to stay the same. We all do it. We all hover. But we don't have to stay there.

O — Ownership Is Lacking

The second letter stands for Ownership — or more accurately, the lack of it. When ownership is missing, we drift through life accepting whatever comes our way. We tell ourselves, "That's just the way it is." But that mindset keeps us stagnant. Ownership is the moment you stop accepting and start examining. Why am I here? What choices led me to this point? What can I do differently? What action can I take today? Ownership is not about blame — it's about responsibility.

Back in the Air Force, there were two teams that paid extra — the explosives demolition team and the airborne team. Both were dangerous. Both required effort, discipline, and courage. Everyone wanted the reward, but few wanted the work. People complained. People made excuses. People wanted the outcome without the sacrifice. I was on both teams — "double dipping" — and because of that, I became the target of jealousy. But their jealousy wasn't really about me. It was about their refusal to take ownership. They wanted the reward without the risk. They wanted the benefits without the effort. They wanted the title without the training.

That's the victim mindset. The victim says, "I don't have what you have because life isn't fair." The growth mindset says, "I can have what you have if I'm willing to do what you did." Ownership is the difference between the two. When you take ownership, you stop hovering. You stop waiting. You stop complaining. You stop comparing. You start acting. Ownership is the moment you step off the cliff and start flying.

V — Vulnerability

Vulnerability is the moment you stop pretending everything is fine and start telling the truth about where you are. It's uncomfortable. It's exposing. It's humbling. But vulnerability is also the birthplace of growth, honesty, accountability, and change. When you refuse to be vulnerable, you hover. You stay in the safe zone — the place where nothing changes because nothing is risked.

I learned about vulnerability long before I understood the word. It started with baseball. I grew up playing whiffle ball in the backyard with my dad and my brother. We practiced constantly — throwing, catching, diving, hustling. By the time we were five or six, we were years ahead of the other kids. They called me "Little Pete Rose" because I was small, but I hustled like my life depended on it.

At eight years old, I was pulled up to play with the nine- and ten-year-olds. I made the All-Star team every single year. My last year of Little League, I had a perfect batting average for the first fourteen games of the season. Then came the game that taught me humility. We were destroying the Pirates — scoring thirteen runs in one inning. The coach wanted to end the game early and asked me to strike out on purpose. I begged him to let someone else do it. I didn't want to get out. I didn't want to break my streak. I didn't want to fail. But I stepped up to the plate and struck out intentionally. It was obvious. Everyone knew.

And that was the day I learned that leadership isn't about perfection. It's about humility, sacrifice, and doing what the moment requires — even when it costs you something. That moment was vulnerability. And vulnerability is what frees you from hovering.

E — Effort

Effort is the bridge between intention and transformation. You can have the best why, the clearest how, and the perfect when — but without effort, nothing happens. Effort is showing up when you don't feel like it. It's doing the reps, practicing the skill, choosing discipline over comfort, doing the boring work, doing the hard work, doing the work no one sees. Effort is the antidote to hovering.

Most people hover because they underestimate the amount of effort required to change. They want the reward without the grind. They want the outcome without the process. Effort is where you separate the dreamers from the doers.

R — Resilience

Resilience is what keeps you moving when effort gets uncomfortable. It's the ability to get knocked down and stand back up, to fail and try again, to face setbacks without quitting, to push through discomfort, to stay committed when motivation fades. Resilience is the muscle that grows every time you refuse to give up.

Hovering happens when resilience is weak. You start something, it gets hard, and you snap back to comfort. That's where the rubber band comes in. Most people treat discomfort like a stretched rubber band — the moment it gets tight, they let go and snap back to their old habits. They recoil into the familiar. But growth requires staying in the stretch.

Cutting the rubber band means refusing to snap back into the old version of yourself. It means choosing discomfort long enough to break through into the life you want. When you cut the rubber band, you stop recoiling. You stop returning to old habits. You stop retreating when things get hard. You move forward — permanently. Resilience is the decision to keep going.

Chapter Summary

Hover is the space between intention and action.

H = Holding Yourself Back

O = Ownership Is Lacking

V = Vulnerability

E = Effort

R = Resilience

Hovering ends when you take ownership, embrace vulnerability, apply effort, and build resilience. Cutting the rubber band is the moment you refuse to snap back into your old self.

10

CONFIDENCE COMES FROM ACTION

Why Confidence Is Built, Not Born

Confidence isn't something you're born with — it's something you build through action. I think back to when I left West Virginia for my first duty station at Hurlburt Field in Florida. I had never really gone anywhere alone, and suddenly I was driving twelve hours by myself to a place I'd never been. I made it all the way to the Alabama state line before exhaustion hit. I pulled into a Shoney's Inn, grabbed dinner, and checked into a room for the night.

I remember how uncomfortable I felt walking into that restaurant alone. I didn't feel confident. I didn't feel safe. I was far from home, far from my routines, and far from anything familiar. My brain was on high alert because everything around me was new. But over the years — after count-

less road trips, meals alone, and solo movie nights —
something changed. Through repetition, I learned that I was
safe. I learned that I could handle myself. I learned that
nothing bad happened when I stepped into unfamiliar
places. Eventually, going places alone became second nature
— something I actually enjoy.

Looking back, I can see exactly what was happening. My
amygdala was hijacked. I wasn't lacking confidence — I was
experiencing fear. My brain didn't trust the environment yet.
That's what the amygdala does: it keeps you alert until it has
enough evidence that you're safe. With repetition, my brain
collected that evidence. The fear faded. The confidence
grew.

Confidence Is the Result of Repetition

This is how confidence works in every area of life. When
you try something new — like playing volleyball — you don't
have the skills yet. You don't trust yourself yet. You're afraid of
messing up, afraid of looking awkward, afraid of failing.
That's normal. But through repetition, your brain begins to
change. Neuroplasticity kicks in. New pathways form. Movements become smoother. Your timing improves. You stop
overthinking and start trusting your body.

At first, you assume you won't hit the ball over the net.
But after enough practice, you know you can. You've built the
skill. You've built the evidence. And that evidence becomes
confidence. Confidence isn't magic. It's not personality. It's
not genetics. Confidence is the result of taking action before

you feel ready — and proving to yourself that you can handle it. You don't wait to feel ready. You become ready by doing.

Real Confidence Is Built in Motion

About six months into my new job in late 2020, the company opened several Nutrition Manager positions. At that point, I had only been in renal dialysis for half a year, but I had been a dietitian for about ten years. Even with a decade of experience, I still didn't feel ready for that level of responsibility in a new specialty. I thought about applying, but I told myself I needed more time to learn the role. I didn't feel prepared.

Eight months later, the opportunity came up again — and this time, I took it. Even then, I still didn't think I was ready. The beginning was rough. I was overwhelmed, driving two to three hours some days, eating out constantly, and I stopped working out altogether. I felt like I was barely keeping up. I questioned whether I had made the right decision. I questioned whether I belonged in the role at all.

But even in the middle of that chaos, something important started happening. During those long drives, I began recording voice notes on my phone. I would talk out loud about the things I had just read — the ideas that resonated with me, the lessons that challenged me, the concepts I wanted to understand better. Speaking them out loud helped me learn them. It forced me to process the information, put it into my own words, and eventually teach it.

Those recordings became my private classroom — messy,

unpolished, honest — but they helped me grow. At the same time, I started sharing what I was learning in a weekly email to my team. Nothing fancy — just insights, ideas, and lessons that were helping me get better. I didn't feel like an expert. I didn't feel like a manager. I just felt like someone trying to grow and hoping it might help someone else too.

Looking back, that was the first spark of leadership. I wasn't confident yet, but I was contributing. I wasn't polished, but I was showing up. I wasn't ready, but I was acting like someone who was becoming ready. Eventually, I learned the job. I started to flourish. I was given more opportunities to lead. I started 75 Hard. I began reading more. I rebuilt my discipline. And slowly, I became the kind of leader who didn't just survive the role — I grew into it.

I wasn't ready when I applied. But I became ready by doing the job. That's what confidence really is — not a feeling you wait for, but a skill you build through action.

Discipline Builds Self-Trust

When you become disciplined, something powerful starts to happen: you begin to trust yourself. Discipline isn't just about doing hard things — it's about proving, over and over, that you can rely on your own actions.

Take waking up early. I don't set an alarm anymore, because I don't need one. Years of disciplined mornings have trained my body and mind to wake up around 5 a.m. without effort. That's self-trust. I don't hope I'll wake up. I know I will, because I've built the evidence.

The same thing happened in Airborne School. We spent hours every day jumping off platforms, towers, and mock doors, practicing parachute landing falls — PLFs — thousands of times. Over and over, we drilled the sequence: balls of the feet → calf → thigh → buttocks → pull-up muscle. (And if you were unlucky: feet → ass → head.) The point was repetition. By the time you jumped out of a real aircraft, you didn't have to think. You trusted your body to do what you had trained it to do.

That's what discipline creates: automatic confidence. It shows up in everyday life too. If I walk into the gym on any given day, I know I can bench 135 pounds. No warm-up, no hesitation. It's not ego — it's evidence. I've done it so many times that my brain doesn't question it. Self-trust isn't a feeling. It's a pattern. And discipline is the pattern that builds it.

How to Create Proof That You Can Rely on Yourself

Proving to yourself that you can rely on yourself takes me back to something one of my military leaders, MSgt Ricky Cook, used to say: "Jarvis, sometimes you've just got to look in the mirror and ask yourself, 'Who's your buddy? Who's your pal?' And then look right back at yourself." Another leader once told me: "Jarvis, sometimes you've got to think outside the box." Those two pieces of advice shaped the way I approach growth. They taught me to constantly look for new ways to improve, new ways to solve problems, and new ways to become a better version of myself.

When you focus on your own growth — when you start

seeing changes in your body, your mindset, your health, your confidence — you begin to build real evidence that you can rely on yourself. Your clothes fit better. Your mental health improves. Your energy rises. People start telling you that you inspire them. But the truth is, you're not doing it for praise. You're doing it for you. And when you show up for yourself consistently, other people notice. They're watching, and sometimes they're hoping to follow your lead.

Think about the times you've seen someone running in the snow, grinding through the rain, or doing pushups in the mud. It gives you something to aspire to. It shows you what's possible when someone is committed to becoming their best. But the key is this: you don't have to live their journey. You have to live yours. Take the pieces that fit your life, your goals, your values — and leave the rest. Growth is repetition and refinement, not imitation.

Trusting Yourself on Race Day

When I want to hit a PR in a race, I study runners who perform well. I look at their pace, their training volume, their strategy. Then I compare it to my own. I don't need to run as fast as them to improve — I just need to understand the bigger picture. What foods fuel me best? How much water and electrolytes do I need? What shoes work for my stride? What clothes keep me comfortable?

I take what applies to me and build a plan around my reality. Then race day comes, and you put it all together. You trust your training. You trust your preparation. You trust yourself.

I think back to 2022 when I was doing 75 Hard and practicing active visualization every day. I wrote out every turn of the race course on an index card and visualized myself running it, step by step. When race day arrived, I felt strong — until around mile 18. I crashed harder than I ever had. I felt like I was going to die. Near Gobbler's Knob, the highest point in Cabell County, I talked with Isaac Wait, who was filming runners with a drone. I was ready to quit. But all those hours of visualization kicked in. All the times I had finished that race before reminded me that I could do it again.

Around mile 27, I collapsed on the ground feeling like death had taken me. My brother caught up, passed me — which was his goal — and told me to get up. So I did. I fought through the last four miles and finished. The next day, feeling awful, I took a COVID test — positive. Later, I found out I also had a brain aneurysm at the time. Looking back, I completed a 50k with COVID and a brain aneurysm. That is all the proof I need that I can rely on myself.

The Bottom Line

Showing up for yourself, doing hard things, and refusing to quit builds unshakable self-trust. Every time you follow through, you create proof. And that proof becomes confidence you can carry into anything.

11

THE FEAR OF JUDGMENT

How Fear of Others' Opinions Kills Growth

Fear of judgment is one of the most powerful forces holding people back. It can stop you from trying, from improving, and from becoming the person you're capable of being. I learned this firsthand.

Years ago, when I was just beginning my self-improvement journey, I signed up for the Babcock Gristmill Grinder Half Marathon. The race started on a downhill, and I took off fast. I lined up with the front runners because I didn't want to get stuck behind people on the trail. As I pushed hard, one of the fast runners — talented, but cocky — started mocking me for going out too fast. He said it while it was happening and again afterward.

His comments got inside my head. I didn't just hear him

— I internalized it. I let his opinion dictate my behavior. What I experienced was an amygdala hijack: fear of ridicule, fear of embarrassment, fear of being judged. A few miles into the race, I mentally shut down. I slowed to almost a walk. I felt defeated, not because of my legs, but because of my thoughts.

I still finished with a solid time, and I was proud of myself. But every time I saw that runner afterward, those feelings resurfaced. His voice lived rent-free in my mind far longer than it deserved.

Eventually, I learned to reframe it. His delivery was terrible, but the message underneath wasn't wrong. In long races, pacing matters. Sometimes you should hold back early. Other times, especially on narrow trails, you should go out fast to avoid bottlenecks. His advice wasn't the problem — his attitude was.

Once I separated the message from the delivery, everything changed. I stopped letting his tone control me. I stopped letting fear of judgment dictate my choices. I started using criticism — even poorly delivered criticism — as fuel and information. That's the shift: you stop taking things personally and start taking them constructively. When you learn to do that, you grow faster than you ever thought possible.

Reframing Failure as Feedback

I always say: If you're not failing, you're not trying hard

enough. Failure is feedback. Failure is data. Failure is direction.

The more you fail, the more you learn. And when you live with that mindset long enough, something interesting happens. Someone asks you in an interview, "Tell me about a time you failed," and you struggle to answer — not because you haven't failed, but because you've reframed failure so completely that it no longer feels like failure. It feels like growth.

That happened to me recently. I stumbled through an answer that didn't reflect who I am. If I were asked again today, I'd say: *"I make mistakes — plenty of them. But every mistake comes with a plan to improve. I learn, I adjust, and I move forward. I don't carry failures with me. I carry the lessons."*

Failure should always come with a plan. Seek out people, books, tools, and experiences that help you grow. Then move on. Don't drag your mistakes into your future.

The Warrior Mindset: Facing Fear Head-On

Fear of judgment is just one form of fear. But fear itself — fear of the unknown, fear of danger, fear of failure — is something I learned to face long before I ever ran a race.

In the military, fear shows up in ways most people never experience. Airborne School taught me that fear doesn't disappear — you learn to act anyway. Every day, we jumped off platforms, towers, and mock doors. We drilled parachute landing falls thousands of times. We practiced until the sequence was automatic: balls of the feet → calf → thigh → buttocks → pull-up muscle. The repetition wasn't just physical — it was psychological. It taught us to trust our training more than our fear.

The Warrior Mindset is simple: **feel the fear, face the fear, act anyway.** Fear doesn't mean stop. Fear means pay attention. Fear means prepare. Fear means step forward with intention. When you apply that mindset to everyday life — running, speaking up, starting something new, changing your habits — fear loses its power. You stop performing for others and start showing up for yourself.

Strengthening Self-Belief Through Visualization

Self-belief is a skill, and like any skill, it can be trained. Active visualization, manifestation, and exposure therapy are powerful tools. Create a vision board of who you want to become — include the actions, the goals, the habits, the reasons why. Visualize yourself doing those things. Then start doing them. Repeat the cycle.

When you visualize a goal, you're already activating new neural pathways. When you take action, you reinforce them. When results finally show up — often on a timeline you didn't choose — you realize the process works.

I think about my garage gym. In 2022, I wrote down the vision: a functional, inviting space to train. I visualized it daily. Now, in 2026, I have a fully functional gym. The rest of the vision — closing in the garage door, adding a window, framing the walls, installing drywall, adding a ductless heating and AC system — is still out there waiting for its moment. But it's coming. I've already seen it in my mind.

That's the power of visualization paired with action. If you can dream it and you're willing to work for it, it's possible.

12

LONELINESS TO SOLITUDE

Loneliness to Solitude

Loneliness isn't always about being physically alone. Sometimes it's about being surrounded by people who have no idea what's happening inside your head. Sometimes it's about stepping into a moment so intense that the rest of the world feels like it's on a different frequency. Sometimes it's about realizing that no one else is carrying what you're carrying — not because they don't care, but because they can't. I didn't understand that kind of loneliness until I lived it.

The Waiting That Made Everything Worse

Before we ever boarded the C-130 Spooky Gunship, we were stuck in Qatar for a week. Not relaxing. Not resting. Waiting. Waiting for the dust storms to settle. Waiting for the green light. Waiting while the war unfolded on TV in real time. Every day we sat in a tent watching CNN. Every hour brought new footage, new updates, new pressure.

Iraq was being taken in the opening days of Operation Iraqi Freedom, and we were watching it happen from a distance — knowing we were headed straight into it. And then came the news about Jessica Lynch. She had just been rescued a few days earlier. Her story was everywhere — every broadcast, every conversation, every headline. It was impossible not to think about it. Impossible not to feel the weight of it. Impossible not to imagine what we were flying into.

That week in Qatar wasn't downtime. It was a slow build of tension, a mental tightening, a constant reminder that the world was changing fast and we were about to step into the middle of it. By the time we finally boarded that aircraft, my mind wasn't calm. It was crowded.

The Flight That Changed How I Saw Myself

I was only a few weeks cleared to return to normal duty after breaking my foot. The bone was healed, but the trust wasn't. Every step still reminded me of what had happened. I could walk, but I wasn't fully confident in it yet — and now here I was, climbing onto a gunship headed into Iraq.

The flight happened during the day, which somehow made everything worse. There was no darkness to hide behind. No shadows to soften the edges. Everything was visible — the ground, the sky, the horizon whipping back and forth through the small windows of the C-130 Spooky Gunship.

I was strapped into my seat in full combat gear — bullet-proof vest, chemical suit, helmet, weapon — with my legs spread wide because a massive combat bag was wedged between them. My knees were about four feet apart, my M16 resting across the top of the bag, my hands locked around it because there was nowhere else to put them.

DeJaynes sat across from me, about ten feet away, also strapped in, also silent. Between us were stacks of equipment chained down to the floor, rattling every time the aircraft jerked. And it jerked a lot. The pilots were dodging whatever was coming at us, and the G-forces hit hard. My stomach twisted. My chest tightened under the weight of the vest. Every sudden movement sent a jolt through my recently healed foot, reminding me that I wasn't as ready as the paperwork said I was.

The plane dropped, climbed, banked — movements that didn't feel like flying, more like being thrown around by something bigger than us. Then the gunner started firing out the side of the aircraft. Real rounds. In broad daylight.

That's when it hit me — not panic, not drama, just a quiet, honest realization: *I might actually die on this plane.* And right behind it came a thought I didn't expect: *Who would miss me?* I was across the world. I had friends. I had people who cared about me. But none of them were here. None of them could feel what I was feeling. None of them could see what I was seeing. It was just me and DeJaynes, ten feet apart, both strapped in, both silent, both processing the same reality in our own heads.

That's loneliness — the kind that forces you to confront your own existence in a way you never have before.

Stepping Into a Different World

When the plane finally stopped and we stepped out onto the ground, my body was still in fight-mode. My heart hadn't slowed down. My mind hadn't caught up. I was still in that aircraft mentally, still bracing for the next violent turn.

And then I saw Spidey and P-Dawg. Shorts. Sandals. Relaxed. Like they were waiting on burgers to come off the grill. They walked up to us smiling, casual, completely at ease — like nothing dangerous had ever happened here.

Meanwhile, I was standing there drenched in sweat, full combat gear on, three massive bags bigger than me, weapon in my hands, still trying to come down from the adrenaline dump of thinking I might die ten minutes earlier.

The contrast hit me hard. It didn't make sense. It felt like stepping out of a tornado and into a beach party. And then the real chaos started. We had to unload everything — the skid steer loader with the fork attachments, the pallet of water, all the gear.

I had three massive bags, each one practically the size of my body, plus my weapon, plus everything else strapped to me. Dragging, lifting, hauling — all while still trying to process the fact that minutes earlier we were dodging rounds in the sky.

I drove the skid steer off the aircraft ramp, trying to keep it steady while the pallet of water bounced on the forks. It felt insane — like I'd gone from combat flight to construction site in the span of five minutes. And then the pallet of water disappeared. Another unit took it. Just rolled it away like it was theirs. We found it days later.

I remember standing there, covered in gear, sweat, dust, and confusion, watching Spidey and P-Dawg walk around like it was a normal day, and feeling something I didn't have a word for at the time. Not fear. Not anger. Not shock.

Just awestruck — at how fast everything had changed, how alone I felt in my own head, and how nobody around me seemed to be living in the same reality I was.

That's loneliness too — when the world around you is calm, but your internal world is still shaking.

The Apartment That Didn't Feel Like Home

This wasn't the first time I'd lived alone. I'd had apartments in the military — but military living is different. There's always noise. There's always structure. There's always someone around, even if you're not talking to them. There's always a mission telling you what to do next.

But when I got my first apartment as a dietitian — my first apartment as a civilian — everything felt different.

There was no mission. No schedule. No built-in community. No one checking in. No one expecting me to be anywhere. Just me. And the silence.

The first night in that place felt heavier than I expected. I locked the door, shut the curtains, turned on the lights — not because I feared something outside, but because the silence inside felt too loud.

I lay in bed and stared at the ceiling, listening to nothing. And that nothing got loud fast. I wasn't afraid of the dark. I wasn't afraid of being alone. I was afraid of the thoughts that showed up when everything got quiet. The doubts. The insecurities. The questions about who I was and who I was becoming.

I didn't have the military to fall back on anymore. I didn't have the noise of barracks life. I didn't have the constant movement, the constant mission, the constant distraction.

I had to build my own structure. My own discipline. My own identity. And that's where loneliness did its real work.

When Solitude Knocks You Down

There was a time I went out for a run on a rainy day. The roads were slick, the air was heavy, and the sky couldn't decide what it wanted to do. I started on the road where it was safe — predictable pavement, steady footing, maybe a dog chase or two, but nothing I couldn't handle.

But like every trail runner knows, the road only satisfies you for so long.

I veered off onto a runoff trail to mix things up, to breathe in clean air instead of exhaust, to feel the earth under my feet instead of asphalt. Before long I was flying — hopping creeks, climbing hills, letting the wildness of the trail wake something up inside me.

I crossed the bridge heading toward Adam's Hollow and started the climb toward a narrow rock formation known as Fat Man's Misery — a tight squeeze even on a dry day. It's a technical section, the kind where you must climb, twist, and jump your way through.

But that day, the rocks were wet. I squeezed through the narrow gap, planted my hand for the jump... and it slipped. In an instant, I was tumbling all the way down the hill. I couldn't stop myself. I couldn't catch anything. I just fell. And for a moment, I genuinely thought I was a goner.

When I finally stopped sliding, I lay there in the mud, soaked, bruised, and stunned. No one was coming. No one even knew where I was. It was just me, the rain, and the reality that I had to get myself out.

That's solitude. Not the peaceful kind. Not the meditative kind. The kind that forces you to face yourself.

I turned back, found the road, and got a ride out of the woods. I was defeated that day. But defeat isn't the end of the story. I went back when it was dry. I climbed it again. And that time, I made it.

Solitude knocked me down — but solitude also taught me how to rise.

The Woods That Broke Me Down and Built Me Back Up

Running long distances will introduce you to a different kind of loneliness — the kind that doesn't care how tough you think you are.

During the 50K, I hit a stretch where I was completely alone in the woods. No runners in sight. No sounds except my breathing. No markers except the occasional blaze on a tree. And that's when loneliness turned into doubt. I questioned everything — my training, my decision to sign up, my ability to finish, whether I'd taken a wrong turn.

The woods have a way of making you feel small, like you're the only person on the planet. But I kept moving. Not because I felt strong, but because stopping wasn't an option.

The Bull Field

By the time we hit mile nineteen or twenty, my body was already falling apart. My hamstrings were locking up. My calves felt like they were being pulled apart. I was thirsty, hungry, and running on fumes. Every step felt like it was being carved out of whatever was left of me.

And then we hit the climb to the bull field.

Calling it a climb doesn't do it justice. It felt like hell — the kind of hill that makes you question every decision that led you there. When we finally reached the top, we weren't done. To get into the bull field, we had to climb over a barbed-wire fence.

Twenty miles into a race, legs shaking, hands slipping, body screaming.

Inside the field, everything got worse. The trail markers

disappeared. The path wasn't clear. It was just open land, tall grass, uneven ground, and the knowledge that somewhere out there were actual bulls — big, fast, unpredictable animals that didn't care how tired we were.

Chris was with me, and we were both exhausted, both hurting, both trying to figure out where the hell we were supposed to go. Eventually we found the exit — but the exit wasn't a gate. It was an electric fence. And to get out, we had to crawl under it.

As we got down on the ground and started crawling, the bull was watching us. Not charging. Not snorting. Just watching — like it was deciding whether we were worth the effort.

I remember the dirt under my hands, the sting of the grass, the burn in my legs, and the feeling of being completely exposed. No strength left. No speed left. No control over anything except the hope that the bull stayed where it was.

That moment — crawling under an electric fence twenty miles into a race, with a bull watching us like we were tres- passing on its land — was its own kind of loneliness. Not emotional loneliness. Not existential loneliness. Just the raw, physical kind where you realize:

No one is coming to help you.
No one is coming to guide you.
No one is coming to pull you out.

It's just you, your pain, your doubt, and whatever's waiting on the other side of that fence.

The Lesson Loneliness Left Behind

Years later, when I look back at all of those moments — the gunship, the landing, the apartment, the woods, the bull field — I see something I couldn't see at the time.

Every one of those experiences was teaching me the same lesson:

I can do anything.

Not because I'm invincible.

Not because I'm fearless.

Not because I never struggle.

But because loneliness forced me to meet myself in ways I never had before.

It taught me what Sgt. Cook meant when he used to say, *"Who's your buddy, who's your pal?"* Back then, it sounded like a joke. Now I understand it was a truth I would spend years learning:

You are your own buddy.

You are your own pal.

You are the one you count on when everything goes quiet.

Loneliness showed me how much I depend on myself — not out of pride, not out of stubbornness, but out of necessity. It showed me how complex we really are as human beings; how much is happening inside us that no one else can see.

It showed me how biologically intricate we are — how our brains, our chemistry, our instincts, our memories, our fears, our hopes, all weave together into the thoughts that rise when the world goes silent. It showed me how much noise we carry inside. How much strength. How much doubt. How much resilience. How much potential.

Loneliness didn't just teach me to survive. It taught me to understand myself. To trust myself. To rely on myself. To build myself.

And that's the real lesson — the one that stayed long after the flights, the races, the apartments, the storms, the fences, the bulls, the silence.

Loneliness didn't make me weaker. It made me capable. It made me someone who can walk into anything — chaos, uncertainty, pain, fear, silence — and know:

I've been here before.

I know this feeling.

And I know I can handle it.

13

BECOMING THE PERSON, YOU ADMIRE

Becoming the Person You Admire

Becoming the person you admire starts with imagining the version of yourself you want to grow into — not a perfect, distant fantasy, but the next evolution of who you are. Your future self isn't fixed. It shifts as you shift. As your thoughts, emotions, habits, and environment change, so does the person you're becoming.

Start with who you want to be right now. What does that version of you do? What traits do they live out?

For me, the person I admire has written a book, is in the best physical, mental, and financial shape of his life, sets a strong example for others, and helps people grow along the way. So I asked myself: *What traits does that version of me practice daily?*

A person in great physical shape trains consistently. They

lift weights. They do cardiovascular exercise. They eat intentionally. They hydrate. They sleep well. They manage stress. They learn through reading, experience, and observing people they respect. They practice emotional regulation. They spend wisely and invest in their future.

Once you identify the traits of the person you admire, you begin living them — slowly, consistently, imperfectly, but daily. Over time, that future version of you starts to take shape. And eventually, you become the person you once imagined. Then the process begins again, because growth never stops. You simply create a new future self to pursue.

Co-Elevation: Working With Your Old Self, Not Against It

Modeling the traits of your future self requires a kind of co-elevation between who you are now and who you're becoming.

Think about the fig and the fig wasp. They survive through a symbiotic relationship — each one depends on the other. The fig needs the wasp to pollinate. The wasp needs the fig to reproduce. They grow together.

Your growth works the same way.

You can't become your future self without your current self. You need the version of you that exists right now — with all your habits, fears, strengths, and flaws — to work with the version you're trying to create. Your future self can't thrive if your current self is fighting against it.

The problem is that most people unknowingly put

constraints on themselves through negative self-talk. They get so used to not trying that they stop trying altogether. They put a lid on their potential the same way the scientist did with the fleas in the jar experiment. Once the lid was removed, the fleas still wouldn't jump. They had learned to limit themselves.

We do the same thing. We cap our achievements. We shrink our goals. We convince ourselves that "this is just how life is."

But what's actually happening inside your brain matters. Low dopamine means low motivation. Low serotonin means you've stopped growing and lost interest in improvement. Stress rises because boredom and burnout take over.

Remember Phil Connors from *Groundhog Day*. Everything changed the moment he changed his mindset. He stopped resisting growth and started reaching for the stars. That shift flipped the switch in his brain — increasing dopamine, serotonin, and the drive to build new neural pathways. He learned new skills, developed new habits, and became someone he admired.

That's what happens when you stop fighting yourself and start co-elevating with yourself.

When you understand the science behind your emotions and habits, you can catch these patterns early. You can interrupt complacency before it takes root. You can redirect your energy toward growth instead of stagnation. And when you do that — when your current self and your future self work together — you stop limiting your potential. You stop living under the imaginary lid. You rise. You grow. You evolve. You become the best version of you.

How to Speak to Yourself Like Someone You Respect

Becoming someone you admire also requires speaking to yourself like someone you respect. That starts with focusing on the one thing you can do right now to improve your life. When your mind is oriented toward learning, growing, and taking action, you naturally begin to appreciate who you're becoming. You thrive. And the negative self-talk that once held you back starts to fade.

Last month, my position at work was eliminated — along with many others. At first, my amygdala fired off like a siren. Shock. Fear. Self-blame. But then I paused. I reminded myself: *I'm not the only one. This isn't personal.*

I stepped back and saw the truth. This wasn't about my performance. It was a system failure — a company struggling with its identity, values, and direction.

Once I separated myself from the situation, I took action. I applied for jobs. I interviewed. I had options. And I chose the place that aligned with my goals, my values, and the person I'm becoming — a place where I can help people every day and add value to my inner self.

That experience reminded me of something important: don't take everything personally. There will be good days and bad days, but how you respond determines who you become.

A growth mindset leaves no room for self-criticism or disrespect. Be your own advocate, not your own enemy.

Daily Confidence-Building Rituals

Confidence isn't something you wait for. It's something you build.

Every morning, start with three things you're grateful for. Write them down. Put them in your phone. Put them on a bulletin board. Gratitude shifts your mindset from scarcity to abundance.

Then identify two or three things you're doing right — the wins you're stacking. When you fail, don't spiral. Have a plan to learn from it and move on.

Show up for yourself every day. Make a list of what you want to accomplish. Rank it from highest priority to lowest. Then start clearing items off your list. Completing tasks gives you a dopamine rush and builds momentum. That's why you start with the hardest thing — the one you've been avoiding. Knock that out, and you win the rest of the day.

When you let tasks pile up, doubt creeps in. When you take action, confidence grows. Do the hard things first. Win early. Win often. And watch how quickly you become the person you admire.

Where You're Headed Next

As you begin modeling the traits of your future self, co-elevating with who you are now, and building confidence through daily action, something powerful happens: you start to realize that identity isn't just shaped by habits — it's shaped by environment. Your surroundings, your routines, your physical space, and the people you interact with all influence who you become.

And that's where you're headed next — into food as fuel, simplifying nutrition so it works in real life, not just in theory.

14

FOOD AS FUEL

Food as Fuel, Not Punishment

Breaking emotional eating cycles takes me back to one of the lowest points in my life. I wasn't exercising. My knees hurt. I was dizzy all the time. A physical therapist told me I had the balance of an eighty-year-old and was at risk of falling. I went to PT, ortho, got cortisone shots — nothing helped. The exercises made me feel worse. My mindset became, *I can't do anything.* And because I believed that, I stopped doing the one thing that always made me feel better: moving my body.

So I turned to food.

Not because I was hungry — because I was avoiding how I felt. I'd go to the dollar store and grab sour candy, sweet candy, ice cream, whatever gave me a quick hit of "feel good." I'd eat whole pizzas by myself. I wasn't dealing with my emotions. I was numbing them. And every time I ate that stuff, I got a quick dopamine hit, a little serotonin bump, and a wave of endorphins from the pleasure of eating.

But those chemicals don't stay long. They spike fast and crash hard.

Eventually, I looked in the mirror and saw the truth — inches added to my waist, pounds added to the scale, and a version of myself I didn't want to be. I had self-sabotaged again. That's when I decided to break the cycle.

I started paying attention to the cues — the urge to grab pizza, the craving for candy, the impulse to escape instead of feel. And instead of giving in, I told myself: *I want to be better. I can be better. I'm only making this harder on myself.*

I replaced the old pattern with new choices: going for a walk, going for a run, eating an apple or a handful of berries. Anything that didn't send me down the same spiral. And I realized something important:

When I was eating junk, the "feel good" chemicals didn't hang around. They gave me a moment of relief followed by guilt, frustration, and disappointment.

So I reached into my tool-belt and pulled out a memory — a time when I was at my best. I printed that version of myself and put it on my vision board. I looked at it every time I walked into the gym. It reminded me of who I could be if I focused on what I could do, stayed disciplined, and just showed up.

That's when food stopped being punishment and started becoming fuel again.

Understanding Cravings (Your Way)

Cravings aren't random. They're your brain trying to solve a problem fast.

- When you're bored or unmotivated, you crave **dopamine.**
- When you're sad or drained, you crave **serotonin.**
- When you're stressed, you crave **endorphins.**
- Food can give you all three — but only for a moment. Then the crash hits.

When you understand that, you stop seeing cravings as weakness and start seeing them as signals.

Ask yourself:

- What am I actually feeling right now?
- What am I trying to avoid?
- What do I really need instead of food?

Sometimes the answer is movement. Sometimes it's rest. Sometimes it's honesty. When you meet the real need, the craving loses its power.

How Food Affects Mood, Discipline, and Confidence

Food is chemistry. It affects everything — your energy, your mood, your motivation, your discipline.

When you eat foods that support your body, you feel better. Your mood stabilizes. Your energy goes up. You think clearer. You're more disciplined because you're not fighting your own biology.

When you eat foods that work against your body, you feel it. You crash. You get irritable. You lose motivation. You feel guilty. You doubt yourself.

Your diet becomes a reflection of how you see yourself.

When you fuel yourself like someone you respect, you start to *feel* like someone you respect.

Breaking the Cycle for Good

Emotional eating doesn't disappear overnight. It fades because you become aware of it and replace it with something better.

Notice the cue

Pause

Choose something that aligns with who you want to be

Repeat

Every time you choose fuel over punishment, you build confidence. You build discipline. You build trust in yourself.

And that's how the cycle breaks.

Once you understand how food affects your mood, your discipline, and your confidence, you start to see that every choice you make is shaping your identity. But food is just one part of the bigger picture.

The next step is building systems — simple routines and

structures that make it easier to stay consistent and harder to fall back into old patterns.

15

SIMPLE NUTRITION
FOR REAL PEOPLE

Simple Nutrition for Real People

Eating healthy doesn't have to be extreme, complicated, or overwhelming. Real nutrition is about balance — balancing food groups, balancing portions, and balancing your lifestyle with hydration, sleep, and movement.

When people talk about "counting macros," they're talking about macronutrients. There are four of them, and three provide energy: **protein, carbohydrates, and fats.** The fourth is **water**, which doesn't give energy but is essential for life. They're called macronutrients because your body needs them in large amounts. Micronutrients — vitamins and minerals — are needed in smaller amounts, but they're just as important.

There's no single perfect way of eating that works for

everyone. But there *is* a simple way to think about food: choose fresh foods more often, and choose less processed foods when you can. If a food has a long ingredient list, I'm less likely to eat it.

Most people don't need strict meal plans. You already know what foods you like and what you're willing to eat. And since I'm not sitting with you, gathering your medical history, height, weight, activity level, and everything else, I can't tell you exactly how to eat — and even if we were meeting in person, I still wouldn't hand you a rigid plan. I'd meet you where you are and help you make better choices from there.

Healthy eating is more than counting calories. There are a lot of extreme diets out there, and you don't need any of them to lose weight or feel better. If you want something highly specific, talk to a Registered Dietitian. But for everyday life, simple nutrition works.

How I Build My Meals

I start with **protein**, add **vegetables**, and then include a **starchy food or whole grain** if I need it. I cook with heart-healthy oils like canola, olive, or peanut. If I buy pasta, I choose higher-fiber options. If I buy rice, I usually pick whole grain — even though I like white rice better.

I also use simple portion guides:

- **Palm of your hand** = 3–4 ounces of protein
- **Fist** = serving of vegetables
- **Tennis ball** = serving of fruit

- **Thumb tip** = serving of fat

Sometimes I use a food scale. I prefer real food over shakes — nine times out of ten, I'll choose meat over a protein drink. The only time I grab a shake is when I'm in a hurry.

I count my macros. I use the 1st Phorm app to track calories, macros, and water. If you want to count macros, work with a Dietitian to find the right plan for you.

Healthy Eating Is Simple

Buy real food. Eat real food. Watch your portions. Don't stress about perfection.

If you imagine your plate like the old MyPlate model, it becomes easy:

- **Half your plate** non-starchy vegetables
- **One quarter** protein
- **One quarter** starchy vegetables or grains
- Cook with **heart-healthy oils**
- Choose **high-fiber options**
- Drink **enough water**

Do this for three meals a day — or four, depending on your calorie needs. Use a food-tracking app at the beginning to get a sense of how much you're eating and check in periodically to stay on track.

You don't need gourmet meals. You don't need rare ingredients. There's no magic food that will suddenly make you healthy. It's the combination of what you put into your body every single day.

If you eat a lot of junk, you'll feel like junk. If you eat healthy foods, you'll feel better.

Hydration, sleep, and movement matter too.

- **Sleep** keeps cortisol in check and gives your body time to recover from stress and exercise. You can't neglect sleep and expect everything else to fall into place.
- **Hydration** affects how you feel and how well your body works. The right amount depends on many factors, so talk to a Dietitian if you want a personalized number.
- **Movement** matters. Weight-bearing exercise builds strong bones. Cardio keeps your heart and lungs working well. Movement gives you those feel-good chemicals that help your mood and motivation.

Food, hydration, sleep, movement, and your mindset — all of them work together to help you become the best version of yourself.

When you simplify your nutrition and build a routine that works in real life, you take a huge step toward feeling better, moving better, and showing up as your best self.

But food is only one part of the bigger picture. To keep growing, you need a system that supports your goals every day — a structure that keeps you consistent even when life gets busy.

That's where we're headed next.

16

BUILDING A HEALTHY LIFESTYLE YOU CAN MAINTAIN

Building a Routine You Can Maintain

Creating a routine around food takes intention. You have to look at your actual life — when you wake up, when you get hungry, when you work, when you're busy, when you have downtime, and what your evenings look like. Life throws a lot at you, so you build a plan that fits *your* reality, not someone else's.

My routine looks like this:

I wake up, make coffee, and add collagen powder for 15 grams of protein. A little cream, drink it, and head to the gym. I lift weights, come home, and eat real food — protein and a high-fiber grain. Then I go for a run. After my run, I either eat real food again or grab a protein drink if I'm rushing out the door for work.

At work, I keep it simple. I either grab something from

the cafeteria, meal prep ahead of time, or throw something together before I leave the house. When I get home, if I've already done my cardio, I think about dinner and usually have a snack — some protein, fruit, maybe vegetables. I drink water throughout the day and, honestly, more coffee than I'd like to admit.

Dinner is usually protein, vegetables, a high-fiber starch, and water or a diet soda. After that, I check my macros and see where I'm at. If I need more protein, carbs, or fat, I adjust based on what I have available. It doesn't have to be complicated. It just has to fit your lifestyle.

Keep real food on hand. Meal prep if that works for you. Eat when you're hungry, and learn the other signs of hunger too — trouble concentrating, irritability, getting snappy with people. Hunger isn't always a growling stomach. Your body needs real food every day, and the amount depends on your goals. If you want help figuring that out, talk to a Dietitian.

Letting Go of the All-or-Nothing Trap

I've fallen for the all-or-nothing trap more times than I can count. Maybe I skipped a workout. Maybe I didn't run. Maybe I forgot to drink water. Maybe I ate a donut.

You have to let that go.

One or two slip-ups aren't the end of the world. If you eat a donut, look at your intake for the day and adjust the next meal — lean protein, high fiber, vitamins, minerals. It just means you're human.

Life doesn't have to be rigid. You don't need the

all-or-nothing mindset. Shift from beating yourself up to advocating for yourself. Get back on track and keep winning. When you adopt a winning attitude, you win more often.

The 90/10 Rule for Sustainable Habits

Sustainable habits follow the same idea: do the healthy things 90% of the time. Be human the other 10%. Enjoy the foods you love once in a while. Plan them into your day and adjust the portion to match your goals.

There's always a way to turn things around. You just need the right "can do, will do, have done" mindset.

When you build routines that fit your real life — not a perfect life, not someone else's life — you create a lifestyle you can actually maintain. And once you understand how to avoid the all-or-nothing trap and make your habits sustainable, the next step is learning how to stay consistent even when life gets messy.

That's where we're headed next.

Chapter 17 is about the compound effect of small choices — how tiny wins, repeated daily, create massive change over time.

17

THE COMPOUND EFFECT OF SMALL CHOICES

The Compound Effect of Small Choices

Small improvements don't look like much in the moment, but over time they create massive transformation. We all want the big payoff — the dramatic before-and-after — but real change happens in the quiet, ordinary decisions you make every day.

Think about the plateau of latent potential. You're working hard, showing up, doing the right things, and yet... nothing seems to be happening. You're stuck in the valley of disappointment. You expect results, but you're not seeing them. You've been working out for weeks or even months, and the scale hasn't moved.

That's when most people quit.

But maybe you're looking in the wrong places.

Instead of staring at the scale, look at the tiny improvements:

- Measure your waist with a tape measure
- Notice how your clothes fit
- Pay attention to the compliments people give you
- Track your energy, your mood, your strength

The "end game" doesn't happen at the beginning. It shows up after the work has compounded. And honestly, there is no true end game — because you're always striving to be a better version of yourself than you were yesterday.

When you're in the valley of disappointment, it's easy to think nothing is working. But if you keep going, the results eventually show up. Those small choices stack up. They compound. And when they do, the progress rises sharply — that's the plateau of latent potential finally breaking through.

So yes — go for your walk.

- Eat the apple instead of the candy bar.
- Drink the water.
- Lift the weights.
- Practice the guitar.

These tiny choices add up to a massive transformation.

Patience is one of the hardest tools to use. We get so focused on watching the scale that we forget progress shows up in different ways. One of the best things you can do is stop obsessing over the outcome. Trust the process you chose. Take the action steps you laid out. Wake up every day and push toward the version of yourself you're becoming.

Imagine this: you weigh yourself at the start of your journey and also measure your waist. Weeks go by and the scale doesn't move — but your waist is shrinking. You're strength training, running, eating well, getting enough protein so you don't lose muscle. Each week you lose a quarter inch. It doesn't feel like much.

But fast-forward three months.

That's three inches gone.

One inch per month.

That's compounding progress.

Small choices. Repeated daily.

That's how transformation happens.

Once you understand how small choices compound into massive transformation, you start to see that consistency is more powerful than intensity. But to stay consistent, you need more than motivation — you need a mindset that can handle setbacks, challenges, and the days when life doesn't go according to plan.

That's where we're headed next.

Chapter 18 is about designing your personal growth plan — a roadmap that keeps you moving forward even when life gets messy.

18

DESIGNING YOUR OWN PERSONAL GROWTH PLAN

Designing Your Personal Growth Plan

Creating your personal growth plan starts with one thing: **your Why.** Before you set goals or build habits, you need to know what's driving you. Your Why is the anchor that keeps you steady when motivation fades and life gets loud. Once you have that, you can start laying out the steps that move you toward the person you want to become.

Start by writing down your goals — both short-term and long-term. Make a list of everything you want to accomplish. Don't overthink it. Just get it out of your head and onto paper.

Most people immediately think of SMART goals. If you've never heard of it, SMART stands for:

- Specific
- Measurable
- Achievable
- Relevant
- Time-bound

It's a solid framework, but here's the truth: when you're just starting out, SMART goals can feel like homework. They can make you overthink everything and stress about fitting your goals into a perfect template.

That's not what we're doing here.

You don't need a perfect formula. You just need **realistic goals.** You're at A and you want to get to Z. There are a lot of letters between A and Z. Trying to jump straight to Z is why people quit.

So instead of saying, "I want to lose 50 pounds," break it into chunks.

Say, "I want to lose 10 pounds," and give yourself six months. Not because you'll necessarily need six months — but because weight loss has its own timeline. When you force a timeline, you set yourself up for disappointment if your body doesn't cooperate.

Think about your vision board. When I was at 188 and wanted to get to 155, I didn't obsess over every pound. I made a skeleton plan. I wrote down where I started, where I wanted to end up, and where I was in the process. I updated it when it made sense. I didn't obsess. I didn't micromanage. I just put the intention out there and took action.

That's the key: **Don't obsess. Just act.**

When we obsess day to day and don't see results fast enough, we get discouraged. That discouragement slows progress more than anything else. Instead of spiraling, pause. Reflect. Then take that energy and put it back into the actions you're already taking.

Your plan is solid. Your direction is right. Don't second-guess yourself. Results don't show up on your time-line. They show up on theirs. The universe has a strange way of making you wait until you're ready. So go with the flow. Don't obsess. Focus on today, not the end result.

Because there is no "end." Every day is a new beginning. Every day is your own personal *Groundhog Day*. Every day you get to be like Phil Connors — learning, growing, improving, and living your day to the fullest. You'll be surprised at what the universe hands you when you show up consistently.

Mapping Your Day

Next, walk yourself through a normal day. Map it out from start to finish. If your weekends look different, map those too. Then go back through your day and highlight everything that adds value to your life and aligns with your future goals. Circle the things that don't.

Right there, you've created the skeleton of your growth plan. You can see what needs less of your time and what deserves more of it.

Identifying Habits and Triggers

After that, identify the things that trigger your bad habits. Be honest with yourself. What situations, emotions, or environments pull you into behaviors you're trying to change?

Once you know your triggers, you can build a plan to replace the old habit with a better one. You're not just removing something — you're swapping it for something that supports your goals.

When you've mapped your day, identified your habits, and clarified your triggers, you can start building your vision. Create a vision board if that helps you. Make timelines. Set milestones. And remember — you don't need to change everything at once. One change at a time keeps you from overwhelming yourself and quitting before the results show up.

Putting the Plan Into Action

Once you know your daily flow, your good and bad habits, your triggers, and your vision, you've built the foundation of your personal growth plan. The next step is simple:

Get to work.

This is where neurogenesis and repetition come in. Every time you repeat a new behavior, you strengthen that pathway. You're laying down more myelin, making that new habit easier to choose the next time your trigger shows up. Eventually, the new path becomes the automatic one — the one your brain takes without a fight.

That's how you build the next version of you.

Not overnight.

Not by accident.

But by design.

Before you move on, take a minute to put this into practice. You don't need a full blueprint today — just the first pieces. This quick exercise will help you get clear on your Why, your habits, and the first steps toward the person you're becoming.

Keep it simple.

Keep it honest.

Keep it moving.

19

LIVING AS THE BEST VERSION OF YOU

Living as the Best Version of Yourself

Living as the best version of yourself is simple — not easy, but simple. You never stop growing. You never stop learning. You never stop choosing the habits that move you forward. Becoming the best version of yourself isn't a finish line. It's a lifestyle. It's a commitment. It's a daily decision to keep showing up.

The habits you've built so far? Keep strengthening them. Keep repeating them. Keep choosing them even when you don't feel like it.

Biology is working in your favor whether you're thinking about it or not. Your brain is full of chemicals designed to help you feel good and stay motivated. I like to remember them with the acronym **DOES**:

- Dopamine
- Oxytocin
- Epinephrine
- Serotonin

You learned earlier in this book what triggers these chemicals. Use that knowledge. Lean into it. When you do things that align with your goals — exercise, connection, progress, challenge — your brain rewards you. That's not magic. That's biology.

And remember: **neuroplasticity never stops.** No matter how old you are, you can create new pathways. You can build new habits. You can rewire your brain. The more you choose the new path, the easier it becomes. When you replace a bad habit with a good one every time a trigger shows up, something incredible happens — the old pathway weakens, and the new one strengthens.

Think back to the anterior mid-cingulate cortex — the part of your brain responsible for grit, persistence, and doing hard things. You grow it by leaning into challenges. Not by destroying yourself, but by making things just hard enough that part of you doesn't want to do them... but the deeper part of you knows you need to.

That's how you build resilience.

That's how you build confidence.

That's how you build the version of yourself you admire.

Even if you start out not wanting to do something, notice

how you feel afterward. That little spark of pride? That's DOES at work. Exercise, discipline, and follow-through all release those chemicals. They reinforce the identity you're building.

To keep living as the best version of you, keep growing. Keep looking for the next step. Keep reaching a little higher. When life gets hard — and it will — it won't knock you off course. Doing hard things prepares you for whatever comes your way. It makes everything else easier.

Growing that anterior mid-cingulate cortex is like building your internal armor. Think of David Goggins — the man is a walking example of what happens when you train that part of your brain relentlessly. Some people even call it the "Goggins part of the brain." You don't have to go to his extremes, but you can learn from the principle: **do hard things on purpose**.

Every morning when you look in the mirror, ask yourself:

Who's your buddy?

Who's your pal?

Who's the one person you can truly count on?

Then look yourself in the eyes and say:

You are.

Because it's true. You are the one person who will always be there. You are the one person who can change your life. You are the one person who can take the next step.

So get out there and attack the day. Start with the hardest thing first and ride that wave of momentum. Never give up on the belief that you can be better. There is no better person to have in your corner than yourself.

The version of you that you've been for years — the one held back by fear, doubt, hesitation, and old habits — is only being held back by one thing: **you.** Your thoughts. Your actions. Your patterns. Your excuses.

The key is simple:

Take the first step.

Then don't look back.

Don't dwell on mistakes.

Don't replay the past.

Don't wait for perfect conditions.

Your journey starts now. And it starts every single day you wake up. Because becoming the best version of yourself never ends — and that's the beauty of it.

20

LEADING LIKE A FLAME KEEPER

Growth: The Culture You Build Within Yourself
Growth is the opposite of complacency. Complacency keeps you where you are. Growth pulls you toward who you're becoming. You don't need to transform overnight. You don't need to overhaul your life in a week. You just need to get a little better — consistently.

If you improve by 2% each week, you become 104% better by the end of the year. That's the power of steady, intentional growth. It compounds. Growth is a choice. Growth is a mindset. Growth is a culture you build within yourself — and eventually around you.

The Recipe for Success

Think of your life like a recipe. Every day, you add ingredients:

your habits

your choices

your discipline

your fears

your courage

your environment

your effort

Add the right ingredients and the recipe turns out well. Add the wrong ones and the result changes. Leave out something essential and the outcome suffers.

Success works the same way. Your "recipe" is the list of things you do each day to become the person you want to be. Sometimes you need to add something new. Sometimes you need to remove something that's holding you back. Sometimes a small adjustment changes everything.

Growth is the willingness to refine your recipe — again and again.

Courage: The Ingredient Most People Avoid

Growth requires courage. Not the dramatic kind — the daily kind.

Courage is:

starting the conversation you've been avoiding

doing the task you fear

facing the person who intimidates you

choosing honesty over comfort

choosing effort over excuses

If you're afraid to talk to someone at work, the only way

through that fear is to talk to them — repeatedly — until the fear loses its power.

Courage is a skill.

Courage is built through exposure.

Courage is choosing the uncomfortable thing because it's the right thing.

Growth demands courage.

Leadership demands courage.

Becoming your best self demands courage.

Building Quality Through Trust

If you want to transform your life — or your team — you must build trust.

Trust is the foundation of every healthy relationship:

trust with yourself

trust with your coworkers

trust with your family

trust with your clients or patients

trust with your team

Trust is built through integrity — doing the right thing even when no one is watching.

Trust is built through consistency — showing up the same way every day.

Trust is built through honesty — telling the truth even when it's uncomfortable.

When you shift a culture from mistrust to trust, everything changes:

communication improves

quality improves

morale improves

accountability improves

performance improves

Trust is the soil where growth takes root.

Servant Leadership: The Engine of Growth

Once trust is established, the next step is service. Servant leadership isn't about authority. It's not about titles. It's not about being in charge.

Servant leadership is about:

lifting others

supporting others

empowering others

educating others

motivating others

caring for others

When you serve others, you build trust.

When you build trust, you build culture.

When you build culture, you build quality.

When you build quality, you build transformation.

Servant leadership is the cycle that keeps growth alive.

The Four Pillars of Servant Leadership

1. Empowerment

Empowerment is for people who lack skills or confidence.

You empower by:

showing them how

teaching step-by-step

giving space to practice

following up to ensure understanding

Empowerment builds competence.

Competence builds confidence.

Confidence builds independence.

2. Education

Education is for people who want to learn.

You educate by:

explaining the "why"

teaching the "how"

giving context

offering clarity

Education builds understanding.

Understanding builds ownership.

3. Motivation

Motivation is for people who are capable but not driven.

You motivate by:

reconnecting them to their purpose

encouraging them

celebrating their wins

Motivation should never be forced.

And it should never be used on someone who is already motivated — it feels like pressure, not support.

4. Caring

Caring is the final ingredient.

Caring looks like:

empathy

compassion

patience

presence

listening

support

Caring is the glue that holds trust together.

Caring is the heartbeat of servant leadership.

Caring is what makes people feel safe enough to grow.

Becoming the Person Who Elevates Others

Growth is not just personal.

Growth becomes cultural.

Growth becomes relational.

Growth becomes leadership.

Growth becomes identity.

When you grow yourself, you naturally begin to grow others.

When you build trust within yourself, you build trust around you.

When you serve others, you elevate the entire environment.

When you choose courage, you inspire courage.

When you refine your recipe, you help others refine theirs.

This is the final stage of transformation:

You stop being someone who is trying to change and you become someone who helps others change.

Chapter Summary

Growth is built through small, consistent improvements — the 2% each week that compounds into a transformed life.

Your daily actions are the ingredients in your recipe for success, and courage is the ingredient most people avoid. Trust is the foundation of every relationship, and servant leadership is the engine that turns trust into culture, quality, and transformation.

When you empower, educate, motivate, and care for others, you elevate not just yourself but everyone around you. This is how growth becomes identity — and how identity becomes leadership.

Choose one pillar — Empowerment, Education, Motivation, or Caring — and apply it to someone in your life this week.

You've built discipline, confidence, habits, identity, and now — leadership and growth culture. You've learned how to elevate yourself and how to elevate others.

The final step is recognizing something powerful:

Everything you needed to grow was already inside you.

In the conclusion, we bring it all together and remind you of the truth you've been proving to yourself chapter after chapter — **you can do this.**

21

THE GROWTH CULTURE: TRUST, COURAGE, AND SERVANT LEADERSHIP

G rowth is the opposite of complacency. Complacency keeps you where you are. Growth pulls you toward who you're becoming. You don't need to transform overnight. You don't need to overhaul your life in a week. You just need to get a little better — consistently.

If you improve by 2% each week, you become 104% better by the end of the year. That's the power of steady, intentional growth. It compounds. Growth is a choice. Growth is a mindset. Growth is a culture you build within yourself — and eventually around you.

THE RECIPE FOR SUCCESS

Think of your life like a recipe. Every day, you add ingredients:

- your habits
- your choices
- your discipline
- your fears
- your courage
- your environment
- your effort

Add the right ingredients and the recipe turns out well. Add the wrong ones and the result changes. Leave out something essential and the outcome suffers. Success works the same way. Your "recipe" is the list of things you do each day to become the person you want to be. Sometimes you need to add something new. Sometimes you need to remove something that's holding you back. Sometimes a small adjustment changes everything. Growth is the willingness to refine your recipe — again and again.

COURAGE: THE INGREDIENT MOST PEOPLE AVOID

Growth requires courage. Not the dramatic kind — the daily kind.

Courage is:

- starting the conversation, you've been avoiding
- doing the task, you fear
- facing the person who intimidates you
- choosing honesty over comfort
- choosing effort over excuses

If you're afraid to talk to someone at work, the only way through that fear is to talk to them — repeatedly — until the fear loses its power.

Courage is a skill. Courage is built through exposure.

Courage is choosing the uncomfortable thing because it's the right thing. Growth demands courage. Leadership demands courage. Becoming your best self demands courage.

BUILDING QUALITY THROUGH TRUST

If you want to transform your life — or your team — you must build trust.

Trust is the foundation of every healthy relationship:

- trust with yourself
- trust with your coworkers
- trust with your family
- trust with your clients or patients
- trust with your team

Trust is built through integrity — doing the right thing even when no one is watching. Trust is built through consistency — showing up the same way every day. Trust is built through honesty — telling the truth even when it's uncomfortable.

When you shift a culture from mistrust to trust, everything changes:

- communication improves
- quality improves
- morale improves
- accountability improves
- performance improves

Trust is the soil where growth takes root.

SERVANT LEADERSHIP: THE ENGINE OF GROWTH

Once trust is established, the next step is service. Servant leadership isn't about authority. It's not about titles. It's not about being in charge.

Servant leadership is about:

- lifting others supporting others
- empowering others
- educating others
- motivating others
- caring for others

When you serve others, you build trust. When you build trust, you build culture. When you build culture, you build quality. When you build quality, you build transformation. Servant leadership is the cycle that keeps growth alive.

The Four Pillars of Servant Leadership

1. EMPOWERMENT

Empowerment is for people who lack skills or confidence.

You empower by:

- showing them how
- teaching step-by-step
- giving space to practice
- following up to ensure understanding

Empowerment builds competence.Competence builds confidence. Confidence builds independence.

2. EDUCATION

Education is for people who want to learn.
You educate by:

- explaining the "why"
- eaching the "how"
- giving context

Offering clarity Education builds understanding. Understanding builds ownership.

3. MOTIVATION

Motivation is for people who are capable but not driven.
You motivate by:

- reconnecting them to their purpose
- encouraging them
- celebrating their wins

Motivation should never be forced. Motivation should never be used on someone who is already motivated — it feels like pressure, not support.

4. Caring

Caring is the final ingredient.

Caring looks like:

- empathy
- compassion
- patience
- presence
- listening
- support

Caring is the glue that holds trust together. Caring is the heartbeat of servant leadership. Caring is what makes people feel safe enough to grow.

Becoming the person who elevates others.Growth is not just personal. Growth becomes cultural. Growth becomes relational. Growth becomes leadership. Growth becomes identity

When you grow yourself, you naturally begin to grow others. When you build trust within yourself, you build trust around you. When you serve others, you elevate the entire environment. When you choose courage, you inspire courage. When you refine your recipe, you help others refine theirs. This is the final stage of transformation: You stop being someone who is trying to change and you become someone who helps others change.

CHAPTER SUMMARY

Growth is built through small, consistent improvements — the 2% each week that compounds into a transformed life.

Your daily actions are the ingredients in your recipe for success, and courage is the ingredient most people avoid. Trust is the foundation of every relationship, and servant leadership is the engine that turns trust into culture, quality, and transformation.

When you empower, educate, motivate, and care for others, you elevate not just yourself but everyone around you. This is how growth becomes identity — and how identity becomes leadership.

Choose one pillar — Empowerment, Education, Motivation, or Caring — and apply it to someone in your life this week.

You've built discipline, confidence, habits, identity, and now — leadership and growth culture. You've learned how to elevate yourself and how to elevate others.

The final step is recognizing something powerful: Everything you needed to grow was already inside you.

In the conclusion, we bring it all together and remind you of the truth you've been proving to yourself chapter after chapter — you can do this.

CONCLUSION — YOU ALREADY HAD IT IN YOU

Thank you for traveling with me through my journey to becoming the best version of myself today. Tomorrow is out there waiting for all of us. My hope is that you take these stories, these lessons, and these examples, and live like Phil Connors — making every day your own personal Groundhog Day. Not in repetition, but in opportunity. Every sunrise is a reset. Every morning is a chance to try again.

You are capable of becoming the best version of yourself. You know your Why. You know what you're pushing for. You know why you want to grow.

Don't settle for complacency by putting a lid on your own jar. The fleas never had a chance — someone else controlled their destiny. But you're not a flea. You're the one who put the lid on, and you're the one who can lift it off.

Start co-elevating with yourself, the same way the fig and the fig wasp depend on each other. Your old self and your future self have a symbiotic relationship. They need each other. Your old self provides the history, the lessons, the mistakes, the grit. Your future self provides the vision, the direction, the pull forward. Growth happens when the two work together.

Every day you make decisions. Every day you choose habits. Choose the ones that move you forward. When procrastination shows up, remember the analogy: eat the frog. Do the hardest thing first. Don't leave yourself with a whole platter of frog sandwiches at the end of the week.

Handle the big thing early and ride that wave of momentum. You can do this. You always could.

Everyone can become the best version of themselves. The energy is already inside you — it just needs direction. Move it. Use it. Let it carry you.

And when you look in the mirror tomorrow morning, ask yourself: Who's your buddy? Who's your pal? Who's the one person you can truly count on? Look yourself in the eyes and say: You are. Because you are. You always have been.

The version of you that's been held back — by fear, by doubt, by hesitation, by old habits — has only ever been held back by one thing: you.

Your thoughts. Your actions. Your patterns. Your fears. But the key is simple: Take the first step. Then don't look back. Don't dwell on mistakes. Don't replay the past. Don't wait for perfect conditions. Embark on your journey now. Because the best version of you isn't out there somewhere — it's inside you, waiting for you to show up.

And you can do this.

AUTHOR'S NOTE

If you made it this far, thank you. Writing this book has been one of the most meaningful things I've ever done, not because it's perfect, but because it's honest. These pages came from real experiences, real struggles, real growth, and real moments where I had to look myself in the mirror and decide who I wanted to be.

I didn't write this as an expert talking down from a mountaintop. I wrote it as someone who's still climbing, still learning, still becoming. Someone who knows what it feels like to start over, to fall short, to doubt himself, and to get back up anyway.

If there's one thing I hope you take from this book, it's this:

You already had it in you.

Everything you need to grow, to change, to become the

person you admire — it's been there the whole time. Sometimes you just need a reminder. Sometimes you need a nudge. Sometimes you need someone to say, "Hey, you're capable of more than you think."

I hope these stories, these tools, and these ideas helped you see that in yourself. And if you ever find yourself slipping, doubting, or feeling stuck, remember this: growth isn't a straight line. It's a daily choice. A daily practice. A daily conversation with the person in the mirror.

You don't have to be perfect. You don't have to have it all figured out. You just have to keep showing up. Thank you for letting me share my journey with you. Thank you for trusting me with yours. And thank you for proving — to yourself — that you're willing to take the first step. Keep going. Keep growing.

And never forget: you can do this.

— Daniel

ACKNOWLEDGMENTS

Writing this book was never a solo mission. It was built on the shoulders of the people, communities, and experiences that shaped me into the man I am today.

To the men and women of the 823d RED HORSE Squadron — thank you for giving me the foundation of discipline, grit, and resilience that still guides my life. "Can Do" wasn't just a motto; it became part of my identity.

The lessons I learned with you echo through every chapter of this book.

To my family, who supported me through every season — the highs, the lows, the setbacks, and the breakthroughs. Your belief in me has always been the quiet strength behind everything I've accomplished.

To Clara Morrell, whose simple conversation became a turning point. You helped me find my way back when I needed it most, and I'll never forget that.

To Andy Frisella, for creating 75 Hard and the Live Hard Program — tools that reshaped my mindset and reminded me what discipline truly looks like. Your work lit a fire in me that hasn't gone out.

To Jeremy Mullins, thank you for pushing me forward when momentum mattered most. Your guidance helped me stay the course when it would've been easy to slip back into old patterns.

To Dr. Blom and Dr. Sheridan, thank you for listening when no one else would. Your willingness to hear me and act on it changed the trajectory of my health and my life.

To Karen Gregory, thank you for seeing leadership in me before I saw it in myself. Stepping into management taught me more about emotional intelligence, growth, and self-awareness than I ever expected. Those lessons shaped the way I lead, think, and show up for others.

To the West Virginia Mountain Trail Runners, thank you for supporting the Kanawha Trace 50K/25K/10K, the Moonlight Madness Night Trail Race, and the Darkness Falls Haunted Trail Race. Your community made those events possible, meaningful, and unforgettable.

To every person who has run beside me, lifted with me, encouraged me, challenged me, or believed in me — thank you. You helped me become the man capable of writing this book.

And finally, to the reader — thank you for trusting me with your time, your attention, and your desire to grow. If this book helps you take even one step toward becoming the person you can count on, then every hour spent writing it was worth it.

ABOUT THE AUTHOR

Daniel Jarvis is a Registered Dietitian, endurance athlete, and leadership professional dedicated to helping people build the mindset, habits, and discipline required for real transformation. After overcoming his own struggles with weight, emotional eating, and self-sabotage, Daniel committed his life to understanding the science of behavior change and the power of identity-based habits.

Through his work in healthcare, his personal transformation, and his passion for continuous growth, he teaches others how to create systems, routines, and mindsets that support long-term success. Daniel's approach blends neuroscience, practical strategies, and real-world experience to help people become the strongest version of themselves.

When he's not writing or coaching, Daniel can be found running trails, lifting weights, or inspiring others to show up for their goals with discipline and purpose.

OTHER BOOKS BY DANIEL JARVIS

JUST SECONDS BEHIND

Just Seconds Behind

Lessons From the Back of the Pack

Most people think the front of the race is where the magic happens — the speed, the glory, the spotlight. But the truth is, the back of the pack is where the real stories live. It's where grit is tested, where identity is shaped, and where ordinary runners discover extraordinary strength.

Just Seconds Behind is a collection of reflections, race-day moments, and hard-earned lessons from the runners who don't quit, even when everything in them wants to. Through humor, honesty, and the raw reality of endurance, this book explores:

the emotional battles that happen when no one is watching

the mindset shifts that turn struggle into progress

the quiet victories that matter more than medals

the identity you build when you keep showing up

This isn't a book about winning races.

It's a book about winning yourself back.

Whether you're a runner, a walker, or someone trying to find your way forward, **Just Seconds Behind** reminds you that progress isn't measured in pace — it's measured in courage.

THE P.A.T.C.H PARABLE

The P.A.T.C.H Parable

A Story About Leaks, Lessons, and Lasting Change

Most people don't fail because they're incapable. They fail because they don't have a simple, repeatable system for getting back on track when life gets messy. **PATCH** is that system.

Born from your own personal transformation, **PATCH** is a practical, memorable framework designed to help people break cycles, rebuild confidence, and create sustainable change without overwhelm.

PATCH stands for:

P — ause and identify the leak

Choose a single, meaningful focus instead of trying to fix everything at once.

A — Accept the challenge

Commit to the process, even when it's uncomfortable.

T — Tackle it one step at a time

Break the goal into small, doable actions that build momentum.

C — Create a plan you can stick to

Build a routine that fits your real life, not a perfect one.

H — Hang up the bucket and examine it for holes

Identify what's leaking your progress — habits, triggers, excuses — and patch them.

PATCH is simple enough to remember, powerful enough to change your life, and flexible enough to apply to any goal — fitness, nutrition, mindset, relationships, leadership, or personal growth.

Inside the book, readers learn:

how to stop self-sabotage

how to build discipline without burnout

how to reset after setbacks

how to create habits that actually stick

how to rebuild identity through action

PATCH isn't about perfection.

It's about progress.

It's about choosing one thing, doing it well, and letting that small win ripple into every part of your life.

If you're ready to stop starting over and finally build the version of yourself you admire, **PATCH** gives you the roadmap.

JUST SECONDS IN FRONT

The Trail Where Legends Are Made

The Mythology, Magic, and Meaning of the KT

Every community has stories. Every trail has legends. Every runner carries a spark of something bigger than themselves. **Just Seconds in Front** is the book that captures all of it — the heart, the humor, the myth, and the meaning behind the KT.

This isn't a traditional running book.

It's a mythology built from real people, real moments, and the quiet magic that happens when a community chooses to believe in something together.

Inside these pages, you'll find:

the origins of the KT and the symbols that shaped it

the stories that became rituals, and the rituals that became culture the emotional truths hidden inside the jokes, chants, and traditions

the way ordinary runners become legends through connection and courage

the mythic structure that turns everyday moments into something unforgettable

Just Seconds in Front blends folklore, philosophy, and lived experience into a narrative that feels both ancient and modern — a reminder that meaning isn't found; it's created.

It's a book about:

belonging

becoming

community

identity

and the spark that pulls people forward

Whether you're part of the KT or discovering it for the first time, this book invites you into a world where stories matter, people matter, and every mile becomes part of a larger myth.

This is the book that shows what happens when a community chooses to rise together — one story, one symbol, one step at a time.

ALMOST A GROUNDHOG

Got it — let's rewrite the **Almost a Groundhog** page so it actually reflects *your* story: a boy, a groundhog, a golf course, parallel worlds, and the mythic-but-funny tone you built.

Here is a polished, book-ready version that fits the real plot and feels like professional back-matter. It will take **1.5–2.5 pages** in Vellum depending on spacing.

Almost a Groundhog

A Boy, a Groundhog, and the Hidden World Beneath the Golf Course

Phil is a kid who loves golf. Shadno is a groundhog who lives under the course. They share the same land, the same routines, and the same obstacles — but they see the world in completely different ways.

Almost a Groundhog is a playful, imaginative story told in parallel:

one storyline above the ground, one below it.

On the surface, Phil is practicing for a junior golf tournament.

Underground, Shadno is training for the ancient Groundhog Trials — a rite of passage filled with burrow sprints, shadow reading, ceremonial tunnels, and the pressure of becoming something more than he believes he is.

Phil thinks he's *almost* a good golfer.

Shadno thinks he's *almost* a worthy groundhog.

Both are wrong in the best possible way.

As their worlds overlap — through divots, burrows, missed shots, and unexpected moments of connection — the story reveals:

how two very different characters face the same fears

how "almost" is the beginning of becoming

how growth happens in small, brave steps

how perspective changes everything

how destiny can hide in ordinary places

With humor, heart, and a touch of mythic charm, **Almost a Groundhog** blends childhood imagination with deeper themes of identity, courage, and self-belief. It's a story for kids, families, and anyone who's ever felt like they were *almost* ready for the next chapter of their life.

Because sometimes the biggest lessons come from the

smallest creatures — and sometimes the person (or ground-hog) you're becoming has been there all along.

THE ALMOST UNIVERSE

The Origin Story Inside CAN DO

Every mindset has a beginning. Every belief system has a spark. Every transformation starts with a moment when something shifts — not all at once, but almost.

The Almost Universe is the mythic origin story woven inside *CAN DO*. It's the symbolic foundation of the mindset you teach: the moment before the breakthrough, the breath before the decision, the space where potential gathers before it becomes action.

Written with Appalachian cadence, quiet magic, and intentional simplicity, **The Almost Universe** explores:

how identity forms in the space between who you were and who you're becoming

how small choices ripple outward into entire worlds

how courage, discipline, and belief take shape long before they're visible

how "almost" is not failure — it's the birthplace of transformation

This story introduces the metaphors, symbols, and emotional truths that echo throughout *CAN DO*:

the spark that becomes momentum

the shift that becomes identity

the moment that becomes a new universe

It's not a separate book — it's the **mythic core** of the CAN DO philosophy.

A reminder that every person lives in an "almost" moment before they step into who they're meant to be.

The Almost Universe shows that transformation doesn't begin with perfection.

It begins with possibility.

It begins with belief.

It begins with almost.

And when "almost" becomes action, a new universe opens.

www.ingramcontent.com/pod-product-compliance
Lightning Source LLC
Chambersburg PA
CBHW060429130626
46555CB00005B/2272